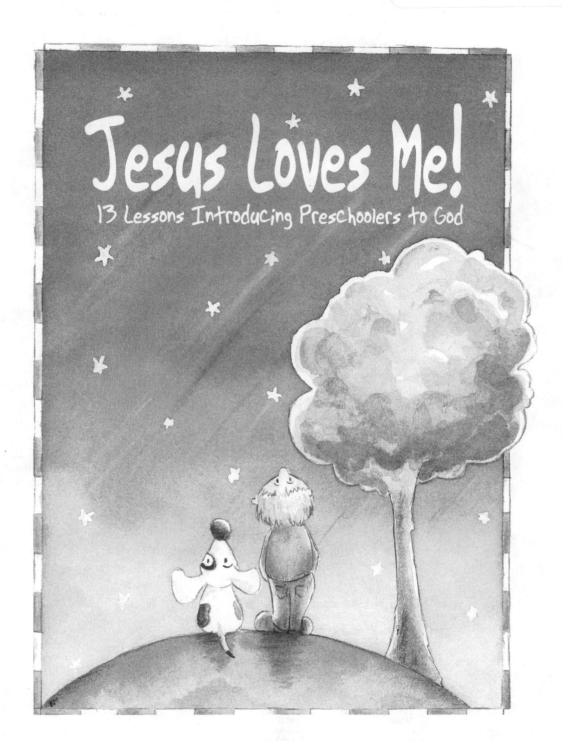

Jesus Loves Me!

13 Lessons Introducing Preschoolers to God

Group

Loveland, Colorado

Group's R.E.A.L. Guarantee to you:

Every Group resource incorporates our R.E.A.L. approach to ministry—a unique philosophy that results in long-term retention and life transformation. It's ministry that's:

This is EARL. He's R.E.A.L. mixed up. (Get it?)

Relational
Because learner-to-learner interaction enhances learning and builds Christian friendships.

Experiential
Because what learners experience through discussion and action sticks with them up to 9 times longer than what they simply hear or read.

Applicable
Because the aim of Christian education is to equip learners to be both hearers and doers of God's Word.

Learner-based
Because learners understand and retain more when the learning process takes into consideration how they learn best.

Jesus Loves Me!
13 Lessons Introducing Preschoolers to God

Copyright © 2002 Group Publishing, Inc.

Visit our Web site: **www.grouppublishing.com**

Credits
Contributing Authors: Jody Brolsma, Cindy Kenney, Barbie Murphy, and Larry Shallenberger
Editor: Jan Kershner
Creative Development Editor: Karl Leuthauser
Chief Creative Officer: Joani Schultz
Copy Editor: Janis Sampson
Art Director: Kari K. Monson
Computer Graphic Artist: Joyce Douglas
Illustrators: Shelley Dieterichs and Bambi Morehead
Cover Art Director/Illustrator: Bambi Morehead
Production Manager: Peggy Naylor

Library of Congress Cataloging-in-Publication Data
Jesus loves me! : 13 lessons introducing preschoolers to God.
     p.   cm.
    ISBN 0-7644-2434-3 (alk. paper)
  1. Christian education of preschool children. I. Group Publishing.
    BV1475.8 .J47 2002
    268' .432--dc21

2002003195

10 9 8 7 6 5 4 3 2   11 10 09 08 07 06 05 04 03 02
Printed in the United States of America.

Contents

Old Testament

Introduction

What's the first thing you want your preschoolers to learn? That God created the world? He did; but why? That Jesus died on the cross? He did; but why? That God answers our prayers? He does; but why? That Jesus rose from the dead? He assuredly did; but why?

"For God so loved the world"—that's why! *This* is what we must first teach preschoolers. If we help children see that God and Jesus love them, they can begin to understand the other basics of our faith. They'll see that because God loves them, he teaches them. They'll learn that because he loves them, Jesus was willing to die on the cross.

Jesus Loves Me! is a book of thirteen lessons that will teach preschoolers that God and Jesus love them. This book teaches children about the characteristics of God and Jesus, and each characteristic is demonstrated in a Bible story. (You'll notice that the names *God* and *Jesus* are used interchangeably depending on the Bible story. That's because preschoolers are not developed enough spiritually to understand the concept of the Trinity. So rather than confuse them, this book emphasizes that both God and Jesus love them very much.)

Each lesson features a fun welcoming activity, an active Bible story, songs, a snack, and a craft so simple it's a snap. (And how many preschool crafts can you say *that* about?) It's called Collect-a-Craft, and it's the same basic concept in each lesson. We provide the art and instructions—all children have to do is color, cut, and create! Each craft also has take-home questions and activities so the learning can continue all week. Get all the details on page 6!

Like the crafts, this book is simple. Jesus loves us. It really is that simple. Teach preschoolers to rely on that love, and you will have given them a priceless faith foundation to build on for the rest of their lives.

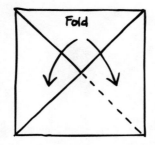

Collect-a-Craft Instructions

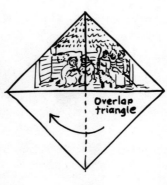

Many preschool crafts either don't look like anything recognizable when children are finished, or they look great because the teacher did all of the work. The Collect-a-Craft is different. This field-tested concept allows preschoolers to create crafts they'll be proud of—without a lot of hassle for the teacher.

For each lesson, make a double-sided photocopy of the craft page for each child. Children color a simple background scene, then fold and easily assemble the picture into a "Biblerama"—a triangular, three-dimensional craft that looks like it took hours to make. Children then add figures from the Bible story to the scene, thus creating a Bible picture that will serve as a review tool for weeks to come. And there's more! Each Collect-a-Craft includes family discussion questions and an activity to help families learn and talk about God together.

So help your preschoolers make crafts they can be proud of and that are easy for you. And don't forget—these crafts keep on teaching at home!

1. Let children color the pictures on the paper.

2. Have children cut out the large square with the colored picture on it.

3. Demonstrate how to fold the top left corner of the square down to the lower right corner and crease. Open the page, and repeat the fold with the opposite corners. Open the page, and cut one fold line to the center of the square.

4. Overlap the two triangles on the bottom of the page, and staple them in place.

5. Have children each cut out the picture(s) from the bottom of the handout, and attach the stand-up figures to the scene.

After each child makes one Collect-a-Craft, he or she will be confident in making them week after week. Encourage children to use their crafts to tell the Bible stories to their families and to point out the family connections on the back. As children collect crafts each week, they can staple them together. Collect-a-Crafts make great review tools, both in the classroom and at home!

The Greatest Gift

Bible Story

Jesus is born (Luke 2:1-20).

The Point

Use this lesson to help children understand that because he loves us, Jesus came to earth as a baby.

Key Verse

"For God so loved the world that he gave his one and only Son" (John 3:16a).

About This Lesson

This lesson will help children discover that Jesus is God's Son and that he came to earth because he loves us.

Children will...

• make "baby footprints" to remember that Jesus came to earth as a baby.

• unwrap gifts to learn that Jesus was a gift of love.

• sing a lullaby and remember that Jesus loves us.

What You'll Need

• Bible
• two-sided photocopy of the "Jesus Is Born" Collect-a-Craft handout for each child (pp. 71-72)
• paper
• at least one stamp pad
• baby wipes
• large gift box
• calculator
• map
• baby doll
• piece of white cloth (such as a diaper or pillow case)
• hay or raffia
• toy sheep
• flashlight
• gift wrap
• safety scissors
• glue sticks
• crayons
• stapler
• graham crackers
• whipped topping
• sprinkles
• plastic spoons
• paper plates and napkins
• self-adhesive gift bows

Preschool Pointer

Younger three-year-olds are just leaving the stage of "parallel play" in which they play alongside, not with their peers. As a result, it can be challenging for them to navigate concepts like sharing and cooperation. Help preschoolers build their relational skills by saying things such as "Let's work together to build a house!" or "It looks like you both want the same doll. Riley can pretend to feed the baby, then Kalynn can rock the baby to sleep." Give children practical ways to share the treasures in your classroom.

Bible Background for Teacher Enrichment

What is your most precious possession? a priceless heirloom? a valuable piece of jewelry? your family? Now imagine placing that treasure in the hands of a depraved criminal. Sound crazy? Maybe to us, but that's precisely what God did when he sent Jesus—his own Son—to be born as a baby in our sinful world. John 3:16 says that "God...gave his one and only Son..." God didn't loan us Jesus. He didn't introduce us to Jesus. He didn't simply tell us about Jesus. God *gave* Jesus to the world as a sign of his indescribable love for us.

It's no secret that preschoolers love to receive gifts. Whether you give them a simple set of crayons or big-dollar toys, children will light up with joy at the mere idea of being honored with a gift. Use this natural delight as you guide children to discover that Jesus was a precious gift, given by God. Help children understand that Jesus loved us so much that ⭐ he was willing to come to earth as a baby to show God's love for us.

Welcome!

Gather children around a table, and give each child a sheet of paper. Be sure to write each child's name on his or her paper. Say: **Today we're going to hear a story about a special baby. Let's make some fun baby-sized "footprints" across this paper to get us thinking about the cute little fingers and toes babies have!**

Show children how to make a fist, then press the "pinky-side" of your fist on a stamp pad, then stamp your fist on the paper. This makes the baby's "foot." Children can press their fingers on the stamp pad and stamp fingerprints as "toes" above their footprints. Let children fill their papers with baby footprints. Then distribute baby wipes, and let children wash the ink from their hands.

Ask: • **How do parents show love to their babies?**

• **How does Jesus show his love for us?**

Say: **Today we'll hear about a baby who was a special gift from God. The baby, named Jesus, loved us so much that** ⭐ **he was willing to come to earth as a baby.**

Bible Story Fun

Before class, place the following items in a large gift box: a calculator, a map, a baby doll, a piece of white cloth (such as a diaper or pillow case), a few pieces of hay or raffia, a toy sheep, and a flashlight. Wrap the lid and box separately with gift wrap.

Gather children in a circle, and bring out the gift box. Let children guess what might be in the box. Ask:

• **When do you get presents?**

• **Who gives you presents?**

• **Why do those people give you presents?**

Say: **People who love us give us presents, and those presents make us feel special. Today's Bible story is all about the best present of all! The things inside this box will help me tell you a wonderful—and true—story from the Bible.** Open your Bible to Luke 2, and show children the words. **It will remind us that because he loves us,** ⭐ **Jesus came to earth as a baby. Our story starts with a man named Joseph and woman named Mary. Mary was going to have a baby. God had told Mary that the baby belonged to God—he would be God's own Son! Let's see what happened to**

Mary and Joseph. Take the lid off of the box. Then let one child take out the calculator. Ask children what the calculator is used for.

Say: A calculator is used to count things. The king at that time wanted to count how many people were in his kingdom. Let another child take out the map. So all the people—including Mary and Joseph—had to travel a long way to their hometown called Bethlehem, where they would be counted. Let another child take the baby doll from the box. While they were in Bethlehem, the baby was born. Mary and Joseph named the baby Jesus because God had told them to. Have a child remove the white cloth from the box. Mary carefully wrapped the baby in cloth to keep him warm. Let a child take the hay from the box. The city was so crowded that Mary and Joseph didn't have a room to stay in. They laid Jesus in a manger—where hay is put for animals to eat! Have a child remove the toy sheep from the box.

Outside the city some shepherds were watching their sheep that night. Let another child take the flashlight from the box and turn it on. Suddenly a bright light shone from heaven, and angels were all around the shepherds! The angels sang and told the shepherds that God's Son had been born. The shepherds were so excited that they ran to worship Jesus, God's Son.

Have children place the items back in the box.

Ask: • Why did God send Jesus?

• How is Jesus like a present?

• Why do you think Jesus was willing to leave heaven and come to earth as a baby?

Open your Bible to John 3:16, and show children the verse.

Say: Listen to what the Bible says in John 3:16: "For God so loved the world that he gave his one and only Son." This verse means that God loves us and sent his Son, Jesus, as a special gift. Jesus loves us so much that ★ he came to earth as a baby to show us God's love. Let's make something to help us remember how much Jesus loves us!

Craft Corner

Before class, make a two-sided photocopy of the "Jesus Is Born" Collect-a-Craft handout (pp. 71-72) for each child.

Let children color their take-home papers. Then distribute scissors, and let children cut off the figure of baby Jesus from the bottom of the page. Help children fold and staple their Bibleramas in place. (Complete instructions can be found on page 6.)

Set out glue sticks and hay or raffia. Remind children that baby Jesus was laid in a manger—a feed box for animals! Point out that there was probably hay and straw on the ground and in the manger "bed." Let children glue raffia or hay to their pictures. Then let children glue the baby Jesus figure to the manger.

Say: When you get home you can use your craft to tell your family how ★ Jesus came to earth as a baby. But right now, let's set our crafts aside so we can enjoy a snack!

Teacher Tip

To make the "gifts" more colorful, you might want to stir a few drops of food coloring into the whipped topping before class.

Teacher Tip

If you don't have access to water, keep a supply of baby wipes for children to use.

Let's Eat!

Have children wash their hands before snack time. Give each child a graham cracker square. Set out spoons, colorful sprinkles, and a bowl of whipped topping. Let children spread whipped topping on their crackers and then add colorful sprinkles to create "gifts."

Remind children of John 3:16. Say: **Jesus loves us so much that ★ he came to earth as a baby. Jesus is a gift of love from God!**

Lead children in praying, thanking God for the snack and for Jesus. Then let children enjoy eating their "gifts" before it's time to sing.

Let's Sing!

After children finish their snack, let them help you clean up. Then teach children the following songs and motions to help them remember that ★ **Jesus came to earth as a baby.**

Rock-a-Bye, Jesus

(Sing to the tune of "Rock-a-Bye, Baby.")

Rock-a-bye, Jesus, lay down your head. *(Pretend to rock a baby.)*

Mary will make a soft manger bed. *(Lay your head on your hands.)*

You are a gift from heaven above. *(Raise arms up.)*

God sent you to us, showing his love. *(Cross arms over chest.)*

God Showed His Love

(Sing to the tune of "This Is the Way.")

This is the way God showed his love *(cross arms over chest),*

Showed his love *(cross arms over chest),*

Showed his love. *(Cross arms over chest.)*

This is the way God showed his love *(cross arms over chest):*

He sent us baby Jesus! *(Pretend to rock a baby.)*

Let's Pray!

Place the lid on the gift box that was used in the Bible Story Fun time. Have children form a circle around it. Say: **Let's thank Jesus for loving us so much that ★ he came to earth as a baby.** Let children take turns praying, thanking Jesus for his love. As each child prays, have him or her place a self-adhesive bow on the gift box. When everyone has had a turn, pray: **Dear Jesus, we're so glad that you love us. We're so glad that you came to earth as a baby. We love you! In Jesus' name, amen.**

Growing Little Learners

Bible Story

Jesus tells the parable of the sower (Luke 8:4-15).

The Point

This lesson will help children understand that because he loves us, ★Jesus teaches us.

Key Verse

"These commandments that I give you today are to be upon your hearts" (Deuteronomy 6:6).

About This Lesson

In this lesson children will learn that because he loves us, ★Jesus teaches us and wants us to learn what God is like.

Children will...

- play a fun game in which they learn motions from each other.
- act out the parable of the man who planted seeds.
- make a craft to help them remember Jesus' words.
- sing a song about how Jesus teaches us.
- pray together to thank Jesus for teaching them.

What You'll Need

- Bible
- CD player and CD of children's worship music
- two-sided photocopy of the "Sower" Collect-a-Craft handout for each child (pp. 73-74)
- large bedsheet or tarp
- masking tape
- small wads of construction paper
- crayons
- glue
- safety scissors
- clear plastic cups
- plastic spoons
- graham crackers
- vanilla yogurt
- red and green food coloring
- raisins

Bible Background for Teacher Enrichment

The parable of the sower in Luke 8:4-15 can help us understand how important it is to be like the good soil in the story. Jesus cautions us that it's easy for the Word to slip away from us. We must be vigilant to let the Word grow in us and not let that growth be hindered by the cares and temptations of the world.

Behind discussion of the soil, we often overlook the fact that there is a Divine Sower. God is in the business of spreading his seed, or teaching us. He teaches everyone, casting his seed on all soils. Preschoolers can learn that God constantly teaches them about himself—through the Bible, parents, Sunday school teachers, and other Christians. They can begin to understand that God teaches them because he loves them and wants what is best for them.

Welcome!

Say: **Let's play a game where everyone gets a chance to be a teacher!**

Choose a favorite praise song from the children's CD. Have children stand in a line next to each other. Choose one child to be the first "teacher." Explain that you'll turn on some music, and the teacher will make up and perform a simple dance while the rest of the children try to imitate what the teacher is doing. After a minute or two, choose another child to teach the class. When all of the children have had a chance to be the teacher, turn off the music, and have children sit in a circle.

Ask: • **What did you like best about being the teacher?**

• **What was it like to be a follower?**

• **What do you think it would be like to be a teacher in real life? Explain.**

Say: **Today we're going to learn about a very special teacher, and that teacher is Jesus! Jesus loves us and ★ teaches us about God. When Jesus was on earth, he told a story one day about how people learn about God. Jesus said the way that God teaches is like how a farmer plants seeds. Let's find out what Jesus meant.**

Bible Story Fun

Before class, lay a bedsheet or tarp on the floor. Use masking tape to divide the sheet into four sections.

Spread the sheet on the floor, and have the children gather around it. Open your Bible to Luke 8:4-15, and show children the passage.

Say: **Our Bible story today comes from the book of Luke in the Bible.** Pass your Bible from child to child, and let them look at it. When the Bible comes back to you, continue.

Say: **In the Bible Jesus told a story about a farmer planting his seeds. Let's pretend that this sheet is the farmer's field.** Give each child a handful of construction paper wads. **And let's pretend that these paper wads are the farmer's seeds. Let's pretend to plant our seeds.** Have children gently toss their "seeds," one by one, all over the sheet.

Ask: • **If this were a real field with real seeds, how many of these seeds do you think would grow?**

• **What helps a seed to grow?**

Say: **Seeds need good soil to grow. Jesus said that sometimes seeds fall on a path and get walked on and eaten by the birds. Those seeds don't grow. Let's pretend that**

this part of the sheet is the path. Point to one quarter of the sheet. **These seeds won't grow on this path. So let's pick them up.** Have children remove the paper wads from the section of the sheet you designated and set them aside.

Say: **Jesus also said that sometimes seeds land on rocky soil where there's no water. Those seeds don't grow either. Let's pretend that this part of the sheet is the rocky soil.** Point to another quarter of the sheet. **These seeds won't grow on this rocky soil, so let's pick them up.** Have children remove the paper wads from the section of the sheet you designated and set them aside.

Jesus also said that sometimes seeds land on soil with lots of prickly thorns that choke the plants as they try to grow. Let's pretend that this part of the sheet is the thorny soil. Point to another quarter of the sheet. **These seeds won't grow on this thorny soil, so let's pick them up.** Have children remove the paper wads from the section of the sheet you designated and set them aside.

But Jesus said that sometimes seeds land on good soil. In the good soil, the seeds can grow and grow! Let's pretend that this part of the sheet is the good soil. Point to the remaining quarter of the sheet. **The seeds that fall on good soil can grow into big, healthy plants.** Children can leave the paper wads in this section.

In this story Jesus was talking about more than just seeds. He was talking about the Word of God—all the things God wants us to learn about him so we can have faith in him. Have children stand in one of the empty sections of the sheet. Have them crouch down like little seeds.

Jesus said when seeds fall on the path and are walked on and eaten by birds, that's like people who hear about God but don't believe in him. Those people don't grow in their faith. They're like the soil on the path. Let children pretend that they're being walked on. For example, they might cover their heads with their hands or yell, "Ouch! Stop walking on me!" Then have children crawl to another empty section of the sheet.

When seeds fall on the rocky soil, that's like people who believe in God for a while but then stop believing. Their faith withers and dies. Have children pretend to be growing, and then have them fall down because of lack of water. Then have them move to the other empty section of the sheet.

When seeds fall on the thorny soil, that's like people who let other things in their lives get in the way of believing in God. Those other things choke their faith. Have children pretend to be growing. Then have them clutch their throats gently and fall down. Then have them move to the last section of the sheet.

But when seeds fall on good soil, that's like people who hear about God and believe in him and never let anything come between them and God.

Ask: • **What kind of soil would** *you* **like to be?**

Say: **Me, too! I want to be the kind of soil that lets seeds grow into tall, strong** plants! Let children pretend to be seeds growing and growing into tall, healthy plants. Encourage children to stretch as tall as they can and lift their "leaves" up toward the sky.

Say: **Jesus said that when we learn about God and believe in him, we can grow up into strong Christians! Jesus loves us and wants us to remember what he teaches us. Listen to today's Key Verse from Deuteronomy 6:6: "These commands that I give you today are to be on your hearts." Jesus wants us to remember to let his good seeds grow in our lives. Let's make something to help us remember that because he loves us, ★ Jesus teaches us.**

Craft Corner

Give each child a two-sided photocopy of the "Sower" Collect-a-Craft handout (pp. 73-74). Let children color their craft papers. Distribute safety scissors and glue. Let children cut the strip from the bottom of the page and then cut out the farmer and plant. Help children fold and staple their Bibleramas into place. (Complete instructions can be found on page 6.) Show children how to fold the tabs on the bottoms of the figures and glue them inside the scene.

Say: **When you get home you can use your craft to tell your family all about how Jesus said that we can be like good soil that lets seeds grow! Remember, because he loves us, ★ Jesus teaches us. But for now, let's set the crafts aside so we can enjoy a fun snack!**

Have children set their crafts aside until the close of the lesson.

Let's Eat!

Before class, dye the yogurt brown by adding green and red food coloring.

Have children wash their hands. Then lead children in a short prayer, thanking Jesus for teaching us. Explain to children that they'll be planting seeds in soil that they make.

Have the children sit at a table. Give each child a plastic cup with one-fourth cup of yogurt in it. Give each child a half piece of graham cracker, and a spoon. Have them crumble their graham cracker into the yogurt and stir it around.

Say: **This will be our soil. Now let's plant seeds in our soil.** Give each child a few raisins. Show them how to "plant" the raisins in the yogurt. Then let children eat their snacks. As they do, invite them to review the story and remind them that ★ Jesus teaches us because he loves us. After children finish eating, ask them to help you clean up so you can sing some fun new songs!

Teacher Tip

If you don't have access to water, keep a supply of baby wipes for children to use.

Allergy Alert

Be aware that some children have food allergies that can be dangerous. Know your children, and consult with parents about allergies their children may have. Also be sure to carefully read food labels, as hidden ingredients can cause allergy-related problems.

Let's Sing!

Teach children the following songs and motions to help them remember that because he loves us, ★Jesus teaches us.

God Plants His Word

(Sing to the tune of "Mary Had a Little Lamb.")

God plants his Word in me *(pretend to scatter seeds),*
Word in me, Word in me. *(Pretend to scatter seeds.)*
God plants his Word in me. *(Pretend to scatter seeds.)*
He wants me to grow up strong! *(Crouch, then spring up.)*

Repeat.

I Am Growing

(Sing to the tune of "I'm in the Lord's Army.")

I am growing *(crouch and pretend to grow)*
'Cause I hear and obey *(cup hand to ear)*
Hear and obey *(cup hand to ear).*
Hear and obey *(cup hand to ear).*
I am growing *(crouch and pretend to grow)*
'Cause I hear and obey *(cup hand to ear).*
Jesus teaches me! *(Point up.)*

Let's Pray!

Have the children gather in a circle. Show them how to crouch down. Have the children offer different ways that their faith can grow. For example, children might say, "Go to church," "Listen during Sunday school," "Read the Bible," and "Pray." After each suggestion have the children stretch up a little more until they eventually are standing straight up with their arms stretched upward. Then close in a circle prayer with children holding hands above their heads.

Pray: **Dear Jesus, Thank you for teaching us so that we can be strong Christians. Thank you for loving us. We love you very much. In Jesus' name, amen.**

Teacher Tip

If children have trouble of thinking what to say, offer the suggestions yourself.

Safe and Sound

Bible Story

Jesus calms the storm (Matthew 8:23-27).

The Point

This lesson will help preschoolers know that because he loves us,
⭐ **Jesus protects us.**

Key Verse

"The Lord watches over you" (Psalm 121:5a).

About This Lesson

In this lesson, preschoolers will learn that Jesus loves them so much that they can trust him to protect them.

Children will...

- learn a rhyme that helps them focus on how Jesus loves and protects them.
- experience a story that shows how Jesus protected his disciples in a storm.
- create a craft that reminds them of the story and Jesus' protection.
- sing songs that celebrate how Jesus loves and protects them.

What You'll Need

- Bible
- two-sided photocopy of the "Jesus Calms a Storm" Collect-a-Craft handout for each child (pp. 75-76)
- masking tape
- crayons
- safety scissors
- glue sticks
- stapler
- orange halves
- pretzel sticks
- cheese triangles
- plastic bowls
- napkins

Bible Background for Teacher Enrichment

The Sea of Galilee was a very large, deep body of water. Lake storms would often come without warning and create violent waves and dangerous sailing conditions. In this story, the disciples were in a fishing boat propelled by both oars and sails. But when a storm assaulted the boat, the sails would have been taken down.

Despite their faithfulness to Jesus, the disciples became afraid. It is important to point out to preschoolers that everyone has times of doubt, fear, and worry. That's why it is so important to help preschoolers discover Jesus' great love in the face of our problems or fear. Knowing that Jesus will watch over and protect us can be a comforting factor as we face whatever challenges pop up on a day-to-day basis.

Preschool Pointer

Preschoolers have lots of energy! Be sure to keep the lesson moving and active without losing sight of your lesson goal. For example, if children are getting restless, take time out to sing an action song. Or you might just pick an action word from the story you are talking about, and ask the preschoolers to perform that action with you. (For example, if the story involves people running, have the children run in place when they hear the word running.) Helping children work out the wiggles in a constructive way is a sure way to keep the lesson on track.

Welcome!

Before class, use masking tape to outline the shape of a simple boat on the floor.

Invite children to climb into the "boat" and pretend to row with you as you teach them this rhyme:

Row, row, row your boat, even in a storm!

Jesus will protect us all and keep us safe and warm!

Sing the rhyme several times with children until they can sing it by themselves. Then let children take turns naming a time when they might need Jesus' protection. (For example, children might say during a storm, in the dark, when they're lost, or when they're sick.) After each child names a time, have the whole class sing the rhyme while pretending to row.

After everyone has named a time, open your Bible and show the children where the book of Psalms is in the Old Testament. Read aloud the Key Verse from Psalm 121:5a: **"The Lord watches over you."** Have children repeat the verse with you several times.

Say: **Jesus always watches over us and protects us. Let's stay in our boat as we hear about a time Jesus protected his disciples during a big storm!**

Bible Story Fun

Open your Bible to Matthew 8:23-27, and show children the passage.

Say: **Today's Bible story comes from the book of Matthew in the Bible. I'm going to need your help as I tell this story. I'll teach you some motions to do and sounds to make during the story. Then as I tell the story, I'll lead you in the sounds and motions. Are you ready? Here we go!**

Have children sit in a circle on the floor, inside the tape boat if possible. Teach them the following sounds and motions.

• When the story mentions wind, children should make a "whoosh!" sound.

• When the story mentions rain, children can wiggle their fingers from the ceiling to the floor.

• When the story mentions thunder, children should stomp their feet.

• When the story mentions waves, have children do the wave motion (as if at a sporting event) around the circle.

Have children practice the responses several times. Then tell the following story, pausing to let children respond.

Say: **Jesus had been teaching all day, and he was tired! At the end of the day he got into a fishing boat with all of his disciples to go to the other side of the lake. Jesus was so tired that he fell asleep in the back of the boat.**

All of a sudden, a big storm blew in over the lake! The wind began to blow.

For Extra Fun

Place the "tape boat" on a blue rug, sheet, or blanket to represent the water.

Teacher Tip

Some preschoolers may be afraid of storms. Reassure them that the storm in your classroom will be pretend. Then take the opportunity to emphasize to children that we can trust Jesus in every situation, even the ones that scare us. Explain that Jesus' protection doesn't mean that nothing bad will ever happen to us—but it does mean that Jesus will be with us at all times when we put our trust in him.

(Whoosh!) **Raindrops began to fall.** *(Wiggle fingers.)* **The little waves on the water began to get bigger.** *(Wave motion.)* **The disciples had to row harder and harder to keep control of the boat.**

Well, things got worse before they got better. Pretty soon the waves were getting bigger and higher. *(Wave motion.)* **The rain was plopping on the disciples' heads as they tried to row.** *(Wiggle fingers.)* **And the thunder was getting so loud they could hardly hear each other.** *(Stomp feet.)* **The disciples struggled to steer the boat. And still Jesus slept in the back of the boat. Then the rain *really* began to fall.** *(Wiggle fingers.)* **The wind blew harder and harder!** *(Whoosh!)* **And the thunder boomed all around them!** *(Stomp feet.)*

The disciples were really starting to get scared. What if the wind blew the boat over? *(Whoosh!)* **What if a big wave washed them all away?** *(Wave motion.)* **What if they were struck by lightning? They didn't know what to do! So you know what they did? They went to the back of the boat and woke Jesus up. They said, "Lord, save us! We're going to drown!"**

Then a very amazing thing happened. Jesus told the wind to be still. *(Whoosh!)* **He told the waves to be still.** *(Wave motion.)* **And suddenly the water became calm. The thunder stopped.** *(Stomp feet.)* **And even the rain stopped.** *(Wiggle fingers.)*

Jesus loved the disciples, and he protected them. And do you know what? Jesus loves you, and he'll protect you! What wonderful news! Let's make something to help us remember that Jesus loves us, and ⭐ Jesus protects us.

Craft Corner

Say: ⭐ **Jesus protects us—that's because he loves us! Let's make something to help us remember today's Bible story.**

Give each child a two-sided photocopy of the "Jesus Calms a Storm" Collect-a-Craft handout (pp. 75-76). Let children color their take-home papers. Distribute safety scissors and glue sticks. Let children cut out the boat and wave from the bottom of the page. Then help children fold and staple their Bibleramas into place. Demonstrate how to bend the tabs on the bottom of the boat and wave, and glue them to the floor of the lake scene. (Complete instructions can be found on page 6.)

Let children blow on the scene and watch as the boat and wave flutter in the breeze, just as the boat rocked during the storm. Remind children that Jesus protected the disciples in the storm.

Say: **When you get home you can use your craft to tell your family all about how Jesus protected the disciples during the storm! But for now, let's set the crafts aside so we can enjoy a yummy snack!**

Have children set their crafts aside until the close of the lesson.

Let's Eat!

Have children wash their hands. Then explain that they'll be making their own boats as reminders of today's Bible story. Give each child an orange half in a plastic bowl. Set out cheese triangles and thin pretzel sticks. Show children how to "weave" a cheese triangle onto a pretzel stick. Then demonstrate how to stick the cheese "sail" into the orange "boat." Have children gently rock their "boats" as they retell the Bible story to you.

After the retelling, lead children in a short prayer, thanking Jesus for his love and protection. Then let children eat their yummy snacks! As children enjoy their snacks, ask them to tell about times Jesus has protected them and their families. After children finish eating, ask them to help clean up so they can sing some fun songs!

Let's Sing!

Teach children the following songs and motions to help them remember that ⭐ Jesus protects us.

Jesus Will Protect Us!

(Sing to the tune of "Bingo.")

Jesus came from heaven above *(point up)*

To love and protect us! *(Cross arms over chest.)*

J-E-S-U-S, J-E-S-U-S, J-E-S-U-S,

Jesus will protect us! *(Cross arms over chest.)*

Sing the song five more times, substituting each letter with a clap as you sing each verse.

Row, Row, Row

(Sing to the tune of "Row, Row, Row Your Boat.")

Build on the rhyme you taught the children in the "Welcome!" activity to reinforce the theme of Jesus' protection. Have children sit in the tape boat on the floor as you sing.

Row, row, row your boat *(pretend to row),*

Even in a storm! *(Make falling raindrops with fingers.)*

Jesus will protect us all *(nod head)*

And keep us safe and warm! *(Hug self.)*

When you get out of bed *(stretch),*

And when you like to play *(pretend to toss a ball),*

Jesus watches over you *(shield eyes),*

Protecting night and day. *(Hug self.)*

Teacher Tip

If you don't have access to water, keep a supply of baby wipes for children to use to clean their hands.

For Extra Fun

Before class, make a pan of blue Jell-O gelatin jigglers. Give child each a jiggler in a bowl so they can launch their boats in "water."

Let's Pray!

Have children stand in a circle. Tell children that as they pray, they'll make a protective circle to represent how Jesus protects us. Explain that you'll start the prayer by praying for the person on your right. You'll say, "Thank you, Jesus, for protecting [child's name]." Then you'll link arms with that child. Then that child will repeat the phrase, substituting the name of the next child for his or her own name. Then the two will link arms. Continue around the circle until everyone has linked arms. Then close the prayer.

Pray: **Thank you, Jesus, for protecting us, just as you protected the disciples during the storm. The next time we're scared, help us to remember that you love us and will protect us. We love you. In Jesus' name, amen.**

A Picnic With Jesus

Bible Story

Jesus feeds the five thousand (Mark 6:30-44).

The Point

This lesson will help children understand that because he loves us, Jesus takes care of us.

Key Verse

"The Lord watches over you" (Psalm 121:5a).

About This Lesson

In this lesson, preschoolers will discover, similar to the way the disciples did, that Jesus has amazing ways of taking care of us.

Children will...

• fill baskets with bread and fish.

• sing a new song about Jesus' care.

• learn how Jesus takes care of us.

What You'll Need

• Bible
• two-sided photocopy of the "Jesus Feeds the Five Thousand" Collect-a-Craft handout for each child (pp. 77-78)
• sliced bread
• tuna mixed with mayonnaise

• plastic knives
• sandwich bags
• paper plates and napkins
• blankets to sit on
• baskets (one for each pair or small group of children)
• glue sticks or glue
• safety scissors
• stapler

Preschool Pointer

Preschoolers love to help with preparing food. It's one of the ways they can mimic their home environment. They also love to work in cooperation with each other. They'll love the opportunity to re-enact the story of Jesus feeding the five thousand, and they'll enjoy the opportunity to serve each other. And in the process, they'll be reminded just how much Jesus cares for them.

Bible Background for Teacher Enrichment

In Mark 6:30-44 we find Jesus and the disciples tired after a long day of ministering to people. They climbed in a boat, hoping to go to a place where they could rest. But when they arrived at the shore there was a large crowd already waiting there. The disciples were frustrated and told Jesus, "Send them away to get their own food." But Jesus had compassion for the people and wanted to take care of them. He asked the disciples to feed the crowd.

The disciples were astonished at his request. But Jesus told them to check around in the crowd and see what was available. Jesus asked the crowd to sit on the grass in small groups and he looked up to heaven and thanked God for the

Teacher Tip

If you don't have access to water, keep a supply of baby wipes for children to use to clean their hands.

Teacher Tip

The mayonnaise in the sandwiches will not spoil in the approximately fifteen-minute time span between when they are made and when the children find and eat them. But if you'd rather, use a different sandwich filling.

If your room is too small to hide the sandwiches in without children seeing, hide them in another room or have children step into the hall for a minute while your volunteer hides the snacks. Make sure your volunteer writes down where the sandwiches are hidden to make sure all are found.

five loaves of bread and two fish the disciples had collected. Then he broke the food into small pieces and asked the disciples to distribute the food to the people. The disciples were astonished at the way Jesus cared for the people because, miraculously, there was plenty of food for everyone—there were even leftovers! Use this lesson to help your children learn that ⭐Jesus takes care of us.

Welcome!

Before class, mix tuna with mayonnaise. You'll need enough to make one sandwich for every four children in class. Place the tuna mixture in a covered container, and keep it refrigerated until ready to use.

Set out loaves of bread, the tuna mixture, paper plates, napkins, and plastic knives. Make sure you have a clean work surface. (You may want to line a table with wax paper or foil as a precaution.)

As children gather, tell them you will be having a special picnic later and you need their help to get ready for the picnic. Have children wash their hands. Then let children help you make the sandwiches by giving each child a job. Children can work in assembly-line fashion, removing the bread from the loaves, spreading each slice with a little tuna mixture, placing the bread slices together to form sandwiches, and placing the sandwiches on paper plates.

After the sandwiches are made ask an adult helper to cut the sandwiches into quarters, place each quarter into a small sandwich bag, then hide the mini-sandwiches in another area of the room away from the story area.

Bible Story Fun

Set out blankets on one edge of your story area, and have the empty baskets ready nearby. Have the children sit in another area for the beginning of this story.

Ask: • Has anyone here ever been on a picnic? What was that like?

• What do you need to have a good picnic?

Open your Bible to Mark 6:30-44, and show children the passage.

Say: Our story today is from the Bible, and it tells about a time when Jesus and the disciples had a picnic. But it wasn't a regular picnic—it was an amazing picnic! Here's what happened. Jesus and his disciples had been helping people all day long. They were tired. Jesus suggested that they all get into a boat and row across the lake for a rest. Let's pretend we're some of the disciples and row our boat together. Lead children in making rowing motions with their arms.

Say: Whew! We're finally close to shore—soon we can rest. Place hands over eyes as if looking far away. Oh my! Look at all those people waiting for us on the shore. How did they find us? What will we do? And it's nearly dinnertime!

Ask: • How do you feel just before dinnertime?

Say: **Let's make growly sounds like our tummies make when we're really hungry.** Lead children in holding their tummies and making growling sounds.

The Bible says that there were lots and lots of people on the shore waiting for Jesus—in fact, there were *thousands* of people! And they were all hungry! Jesus and his disciples got out of the boat and walked up on the hillside. Have children stand up and slowly walk to the area where you placed the blankets. Direct the children to sit on the blankets. The disciples were talking to each other and saying, "How can we take care of all these people? What will we feed them?" Finally, the disciples went to Jesus and said, "This place is in the middle of nowhere and it's getting late. Maybe you'd better send all these people away so they can walk to a town and get some food."

But Jesus had another idea! Jesus told the disciples, "*You* give them something to eat."

Ask: • **What do you think the disciples thought about that?**

• **How would you feel if you suddenly had to feed five thousand people? What would you do?**

• **What do you think the disciples said and did?**

Say: **Well, the disciples had no idea what to do! They said to Jesus, "But that would take eight months of pay to buy that much food. No way! We don't have enough food!"**

Stand up and go individually to the children and ask them, "**Do *you* have any food?**" Wait for responses and then return to the story.

Say: **Just as you don't have any food to share, the disciples didn't have any food either. But they knew that ⭐ Jesus takes care of us, so they listened to what he said next. Jesus asked how much food they had, and the disciples went to find out. Let's be like the disciples. Let's go find out how much food we have! There are little sandwiches hidden in our room. Let's go look for them. Collect them in your baskets and meet me at the snack area.**

Show children the baskets, and encourage them to find the sandwiches your volunteer hid earlier. When all of the sandwiches have been found, collect the baskets. Have children gather near the blankets, and continue with the next part of the lesson.

Let's Eat!

Have children wash their hands. Hold up the baskets the children collected.

Say: **The disciples came back to Jesus and reported that they had five loaves of bread and two fish. Surely that wouldn't be enough to feed five thousand people! But we know that ⭐ Jesus takes care of us, so let's find out what happened next.**

Jesus told the people to sit down in groups on the green grass. Let's sit down too.

Teacher Tip

If you don't have access to water, keep a supply of baby wipes for children to use.

23

Have children sit on the floor in your "picnic" area. **Jesus took the fish and loaves and looked up to heaven. He prayed to thank God for the food. Let's thank God for *our* food too!** Lead children in a short prayer of thanksgiving for the food they collected. **After Jesus prayed, he handed the food to the disciples to give to the people in the crowd.** Distribute napkins and the mini-sandwiches to the children.

As the disciples handed out the food, something amazing happened. Those five loaves of bread and two fish turned into enough food to feed everyone there that day! That's five thousand people! And that's not all—there were even leftovers! All of the people had plenty to eat and weren't hungry anymore. **Let's eat our yummy snack too!** As children enjoy their sandwiches, ask the following questions.

Ask: • How could five loaves and two fish feed thousands of people?

• Why do you think Jesus wanted to feed all those people?

Say: **Jesus performed a miracle when he made that little bit of food feed five thousand people! Jesus took care of the five thousand people because he loved them. And ⭐ Jesus takes care of us because he loves us too! Listen to what the Bible says in verse Psalm 121:5 about how Jesus cares for us: "The Lord watches over you"** Have children repeat the verse with you several times. **Jesus always cares for us. That's because he loves us! Let's make something to help us remember that ⭐ Jesus always takes care of us.**

Let children help you clean up after the snack. Then move on to the craft activity.

Craft Corner

Give each child a two-sided photocopy of the "Jesus Feeds the Five Thousand" Collect-a-Craft handout (pp. 77-78). Let children color their take-home papers. Set out safety scissors and glue to share. Show children how to cut off the bottom portion of their pages. Then help children fold and staple their Biblerama into place. (Complete instructions can be found on page 6.) Then let children glue the fish and loaves to their pictures.

Say: **When you get home, you can use this craft to tell your family all about how Jesus fed those five thousand people. And be sure to tell them that because he loves us, ⭐ Jesus takes care of us! But before we go, let's sing a few fun songs about today's Bible story.**

Let's Sing!

Teach children the following songs and motions to help them remember that because he loves us, ⭐ Jesus takes care of us.

Jesus Feeds the Five Thousand

(Sing to the tune of "Jesus Loves the Little Children.")

How did Jesus feed the hungry people? *(Hold hands palms up and shrug.)*

There were five thousand, give or take a few. *(Hold up five fingers.)*

Jesus prayed to God above *(make praying hands),*

Then he showed them all his love. *(Hug self.)*

Jesus cared for them, and he will care for you! *(Point to others.)*

Jesus Cares for Us

(Sing to the tune of "The Farmer in the Dell.")

Have children hold hands in a circle. Move around in a circle as you sing this song. When children sing the third line of each verse, have them drop hands and hug themselves.

Jesus cares for us.

Jesus cares for us.

Hi-ho, he loves us so.

Jesus cares for us.

He fed the hungry crowd.

He fed the hungry crowd.

Hi-ho, he loved them so.

He fed the hungry crowd.

Teacher Tip

As you sing this song with the children, personalize it by singing a verse for each child in the class. For example, "Jesus cares for Todd."

Let's Pray!

Ask children to tell you what some of their favorite foods are, then have them bow their heads. Ask each child to thank Jesus for his or her favorite food in a one-sentence prayer. Then have everyone say together, "Thank you, Jesus, for taking care of us." Continue until each child has had a turn to thank Jesus personally. Then close the prayer yourself, thanking Jesus for taking care of the children in your class.

A Father's Forgiveness

Bible Story

Jesus tells the parable of the lost son (Luke 15:11-32).

The Point

This lesson will help children understand that because he loves us, ⭐ **God forgives us.**

Key Verse

"Forgive as the Lord forgave you" (Colossians 3:13b).

About This Lesson

In this lesson, preschoolers will be encouraged as they learn about a son whose father forgave him and welcomed him home.

Children will...

- have a Forgiveness Festival.
- sing the Bible story.
- learn that God forgives us.
- thank Jesus for his forgiveness.

What You'll Need

- Bible
- two-sided photocopy of the "Lost Son" Collect-a-Craft handout for each child (pp. 79-80)
- brown paint or real mud
- crayons
- colored construction paper cut for party hats
- safety scissors
- stapler
- glue sticks or glue
- tape
- glitter glue
- colored markers
- baby wipes
- graham crackers
- white frosting or soft cream cheese
- colored sprinkles
- plastic knives
- paper plates and napkins

Bible Background for Teacher Enrichment

The story of the lost son in Luke 15:11-32 is understandable for young children because their everyday experiences are mainly in the context of family relationships. This is a story about a son who leaves home and messes up his life, and about the father who forgives him.

The younger of the father's sons requested his inheritance, demonstrating that his heart was no longer "at home" with his father but was focused on the freedom the money would offer. The son foolishly squandered his inheritance and was reduced to near starvation and the degradation of working in a pigsty.

Preschool Pointer

Your preschoolers have a high view of themselves and are sometimes convinced they can do no wrong. Today's Bible story helps to point out that everyone does wrong things and has a need for forgiveness from other family members, as well as from God. Use this story to convince your preschoolers that they are in need of forgiveness and that it is available to them because of Jesus.

It was then that he realized how wrong he had been, and he vowed to go home and throw himself on his father's mercy.

It's interesting to note that the father *ran* to meet his son on the road. A wealthy landowner would never have run anywhere and would normally have had his servants greet a visitor on the road. Instead, we see the joy the father had in receiving his son home again. What a wonderful picture of our God, who waits for us, ready to forgive us completely when we repent of our sins!

Welcome!

Before class, cut construction paper to make party hats for the children. For each hat, cut a sheet of construction paper into a large triangle with one of the sides curved out. Children will decorate the hats while they're flat. Then for each hat, you'll staple the two straight sides together to form a cone-shaped hat. Use the margin illustration as a guide.

As children arrive, tell them that you'll be having a Forgiveness Festival later in the lesson and that you'll need their help getting ready for it. Set out the pre-cut construction paper, glitter glue, colored markers, and crayons. Encourage each child to decorate a party hat with the supplies you provided. Then staple the sides of each child's triangle together to form a hat. Help children write their names on the hats, and set the hats aside to wear at the Forgiveness Festival.

staple here

Bible Story Fun

You'll teach today's Bible story as a call-and-response song. To set it up, summarize the story in the following way.

Say: **I want to tell you about a story in the Bible.** Open your Bible to Luke 15:11-32, and show the children the passage. **This story is found in the book of Luke in the Bible. It's a story that Jesus told to teach us about forgiving each other. This story is about a son who ran away, but whose father forgave him when he came back.**

Instead of just telling you the story, I'm going to sing it! I'll sing a line, and you can sing the line back to me. I'll even show you some motions to do. OK? Let's sing our story!

Sing the following story song to the tune of "Where, Oh Where, Has My Little Dog Gone?" You'll sing a line and do the motions, then lead the children in repeating the line and motions.

Where, oh where, has my younger son gone? *(Hands shading eyes.)*
Where, oh where, can he be? *(Hands shading eyes.)*
He took all his money and went away. *(Walk in place.)*
I wish he'd come right back to me. *(Beckon "come back.")*

He went away, and he spent all he had. *(Show empty hands.)*

He spent all the money he had. *(Show empty hands.)*

He went away, and he spent all he had. *(Show empty hands.)*

And now things were looking bad. *(Shake head side to side.)*

He got a job in a field full of pigs. *(Hold nose.)*

Oh my, oh my, it did stink! *(Hold nose.)*

He got a job in a field full of pigs. *(Hold nose.)*

And then he started to think. *(Point to head.)*

"I want to go home and see my dad." *(Pretend to cry.)*

"I want to go home right away." *(Pretend to cry.)*

"I want to go home and see my dad." *(Pretend to cry.)*

"I'll leave this pigpen right away!" *(Nod head.)*

He left all those pigs, and he started for home. *(Walk in place.)*

At home, he wanted to live. *(Walk in place.)*

He left all those pigs, and he started for home. *(Walk in place.)*

But would his father forgive? *(Rub chin.)*

His father saw him and ran to him. *(Run in place.)*

He ran along the path. *(Run in place.)*

His father saw him and ran to him. *(Run in place.)*

And then they both started to laugh. *(Hold belly and laugh.)*

"Oh Father, Father, I'm sorry I left." *(Clasp hands.)*

"Can you please forgive me?" *(Clasp hands.)*

"Oh Son, oh Son, I am so glad you're home." *(Clap hands.)*

"I'll forgive you, just wait and see!" *(Clap hands and nod.)*

The father had a party to celebrate. *(Jump in place.)*

His son had come home to live. *(Rest head on hands.)*

The son joined the party to celebrate. *(Jump in place.)*

He learned that his father forgives. *(Cross arms over chest.)*

After the song, lead children in a round of applause for their participation. Then let everyone sit down for a rest!

Ask: • How did the father feel when his son left home?

• How did the son feel when he had spent all his money and was working in the pigpen?

• Why did the son want to go home?

• Why did the father forgive his son?

Say: The father forgave his son because he loved him! And that's why ★ God forgives us—because he loves us. God sent his Son, Jesus, so we could be forgiven for our sins. When we believe in Jesus, God will forgive our sins. Sometimes we do things we shouldn't, just like the son in this story. But we can always go to God and ask him to forgive us. And just like the father in this story, ⭐ God forgives us.

Craft Corner

Give each child a two-sided photocopy of the "Lost Son" Collect-a-Craft handout (pp. 79-80). Let children color their craft papers. Distribute scissors and glue. Let children cut out the father and son figures from the bottom of the page. Then help children fold and staple their Bibleramas into place. (Complete instructions can be found on page 6.) Show the children how to fold the tabs on the bottom of the father and son figures and glue them inside the scene.

Set out the brown paint or mud, and let each child dip a finger or thumb into the paint or mud and make smudges on the son and the pigs in the picture. Have the children leave their fingers "dirty" and go to prayer time next.

Say: **When you get home you can use your craft to tell your family all about how the son left home and the father forgave him when he came back. You can use your craft to remind you that because he loves us,** ⭐ **God forgives us. Right now, let's see what it's like to be forgiven.**

Have the children set their crafts aside until the close of the lesson. Children will clean their hands off in the next activity.

Let children decorate their crafts with glitter glue and curled ribbon taped to the scene to remind them of the party the father had to celebrate the return of his son.

Let's Pray!

Have the children sit in a circle on the floor.

Say: **Your hands look really dirty.**

Ask: **What do you do when your hands are dirty?** Wait for answers.

Say: **When our hands are dirty, we like to wash that dirt off. When we sin, or do wrong things, it's like our hearts get dirty. The only way to get our hearts clean again is to believe in Jesus and ask God to forgive us. I have a baby wipe for each one of you. When you wipe off your hands I want you to think of one thing you've done wrong lately. Then, as you're wiping the dirt off your hands say, "Thank you, God, for forgiving me."**

Go around the circle and give each child a baby wipe and let children wipe their hands as they pray. Open your Bible to Colossians 3:13b, and show children the Key Verse. Then read aloud the verse: **"Forgive as the Lord forgave you."** Explain that because ⭐ God forgives us, we can forgive others. Ask each child to think of someone he or she can forgive in the coming week. Then close the prayer by thanking God for loving us and forgiving us, just as the father in the story loved and forgave his son.

Let's Eat!

Say: **Remember how I said we'd be having a Forgiveness Festival? Let's put on our party hats!**

Have the children retrieve the party hats they made earlier and put them on. Set out graham crackers, white frosting or cream cheese, and colored sprinkles.

Say: **The graham cracker looks dirty like sin, or the wrong things we do.** Give each child a graham cracker on a paper plate. **When God forgives us, we're clean and our sins are all gone. Let's cover these graham crackers with white frosting to remind us that our sins disappear when God forgives us.** Let children spread frosting on their crackers. **These sprinkles can remind us of the party the father in our story had when his son came home. Let's add party sprinkles to our snacks!** Let children add sprinkles.

Lead children in a short prayer of thanksgiving for the snacks, then let them enjoy their treats. As children eat, remind them that because he loves us, ⭐ God forgives us. Then ask children to help you clean up so you can sing some fun songs!

Let's Sing!

Let children keep the party hats on as you teach them the words and motions to the following songs.

God Forgives Me!

(Sing to the tune of "Jesus Loves Me.")

God forgives me, this I know *(pretend to wash hands)*
For the Bible tells me so. *(Open palms as if reading)*
When I come to him in prayer *(make praying hands),*
I know that he always cares. *(Cross arms over chest.)*
Yes, he forgives me! *(Pretend to wash hands.)*
Yes, he forgives me! *(Pretend to wash hands.)*
Yes, he forgives me *(pretend to wash hands)*
Because he loves me so! *(Hug self.)*

Repeat.

I Am Forgiven!

(Sing to the tune of "I've Got the Joy, Joy, Joy, Joy.")

I know that God forgives me, down in my heart *(hands over heart),*
Down in my heart, down in my heart. *(Hands over heart.)*
I know that God forgives me, down in my heart. *(Hands over heart.)*
I am forgiven today. Hooray! *(Jump and clap.)*

Repeat.

Looking Down on Forgiveness

Bible Story

Jesus talks to Zacchaeus (Luke 19:1-10).

The Point

This lesson will help children understand that ⭐ **God forgives us.**

Key Verse

"Forgive as the Lord forgave you" (Colossians 3:13b).

About This Lesson

Use this lesson to help children understand how forgiving God is with us and how they can be forgiving with others.

Children will...

• use "binoculars" to try to see Jesus.

• sing a new song about forgiveness.

• learn how Jesus forgives us and how we can forgive others.

What You'll Need

- Bible
- two-sided photocopy of "Zacchaeus" Collect-a-Craft handout (pp. 81-82) for each child
- cardboard tubes cut to 4½ inches
- colored masking tape
- picture of Jesus
- tree twig (8-10 inches long) for each child
- glue sticks or glue
- safety scissors
- stapler
- plain white construction paper
- frosting
- vanilla wafers
- paper plates and napkins

Preschool Pointer

Preschool children have moved from parallel play (playing next to each other without really engaging one another) to interactive play with their friends. Invariably, conflict over possessions and play space will arise. It's so important to help these little ones who are new at relationship building to learn to ask for forgiveness when they have hurt a friend and to learn to give forgiveness when a friend has hurt them. Use this lesson about Jesus' forgiveness of Zacchaeus to teach the basic concept of how ⭐ God forgives us.

Bible Background for Teacher Enrichment

There's something about the story of Zacchaeus that young children love. Maybe they like to imagine the awkward picture of a grown man holding on to a tree branch. More likely, children can identify with Zacchaeus. Preschoolers often strain to get a better view of a world that caters to grown-ups. Like Zacchaeus, young children just want to be a part of things—they want to be included in what God is doing.

How wonderful that we get to give children the message they long to hear. What a privilege it is to tell children that they are important to God and that the message of grace and forgiveness is every bit as much for them as it is for adults. Jesus gladly forgave and accepted Zacchaeus, who was shunned because of his greed. Use the story to help children see that Jesus also gladly forgives and accepts them.

Welcome!

Welcome children by bending down to their level and saying their names with a smile.

Say: **Today we're going to learn about a man named Zacchaeus who wanted to see Jesus. Zacchaeus was really short. But that isn't why people didn't like him very much. People didn't like him because he was a tax collector. There were so many people around Jesus that Zacchaeus never had a chance to see Jesus. Let's play a game that shows us what it may have been like for Zacchaeus.**

Ask for a volunteer to be "Zacchaeus." Have the other children form a tight circle. Direct Zacchaeus to stand outside the circle while you stand in the middle. Have Zacchaeus try to find a way into the middle of the circle. Zacchaeus can try to gently push his or her way through, quickly find an opening, or ask others to let him or her in.

If Zacchaeus isn't successful in getting in, say: **Zacchaeus climbed a tree to see Jesus. When Jesus saw Zacchaeus, he told the short man to get down so they could talk and have dinner together. Let's open up the circle so Zacchaeus can come in.**

When Zacchaeus gets into the middle of the circle, have all the children give Zacchaeus a gentle hug, and say: **We're glad you're here, Zacchaeus.**

Play again allowing children to take turns being Zacchaeus.

Say: **Jesus wanted to be with Zacchaeus just like Jesus wants to be with you. We're going to take some time to learn more about how Jesus loved and forgave Zacchaeus and how ⭐ God forgives us.**

Bible Story Fun

Direct children to make their own "binoculars." Set out cardboard tubes and colored masking tape. Assist children in taping together two of the tubes to make binoculars. Tell children they will be using their binoculars to look for Jesus, just as Zacchaeus looked for Jesus.

Tape a picture of Jesus on the floor under a table. Tell the children there is a picture of Jesus somewhere in the room. Ask them to use their binoculars to find it.

After most of the children have seen the picture, ask them to sit in a circle near the table where the picture of Jesus is.

Ask: • **How did you find Jesus?**

• **Did any of you have a tough time seeing Jesus?**

Say: **I'm opening my Bible to Luke 19:1-10 to tell you the story of Zacchaeus. Zacchaeus had a hard time trying to see Jesus too. Jesus was walking along a road. The whole town was excited about seeing Jesus so they had gathered to welcome Jesus. Zacchaeus was short, and he couldn't see Jesus over the crowd. Zacchaeus had** also taken money from some of these people. They were mad at Zacchaeus so they weren't going to let him in front of them to see Jesus.

He tried jumping up higher. Let's all try jumping up to make ourselves taller. Did that work? I guess not. Zacchaeus tried to move back and forth to see between the people in the crowd. Let's all bend forward and move back and forth to see if we can see better. Did that work? I don't think so. Zacchaeus tried crawling on the floor so he could see between their legs. Let's all crawl and see if that helps us see Jesus. Did crawling help? No, not really.

Ask: • What would you do if you couldn't see Jesus through a crowd of people?

• How do you think Zacchaeus could get to see Jesus?

Say: Zacchaeus climbed a tree so he could see over the crowd. Let's pretend to climb into a tree. While Zacchaeus was looking at Jesus, over the heads of the crowd, Jesus stopped and looked up at him. Let's all look down from our tree limbs to see Jesus.

Ask: • How do you think Zacchaeus felt when Jesus looked up at him?

• If you knew you had done wrong things by taking money that wasn't really yours, how would it feel to look into the eyes of Jesus?

Say: Jesus didn't get mad at Zacchaeus. He didn't make fun of Zacchaeus. Jesus just told Zacchaeus to get down from the tree so they could have dinner together. Let's all climb down from our trees. Now grab someone else's hand the way Zacchaeus may have held Jesus' hand.

Zacchaeus was so honored that Jesus would want to come to his house with him. Because Zacchaeus had done some wrong things, like taking money that didn't really belong to him, nobody liked Zacchaeus anymore. He didn't have any friends. When Zacchaeus spent time with Jesus, he knew that he had been doing wrong things. Jesus told Zacchaeus that he had come to find lost people who needed forgiveness. God sent Jesus to visit with lost people who needed forgiveness because ⭐ God forgives us. Jesus showed Zacchaeus how much God loved him and forgave him. Zacchaeus was so sorry for what he had done and so thankful that Jesus was willing to forgive him.

Let's all bow our heads and think of wrong things we have done. No matter what we have done, ⭐ God forgives us when we ask him to. Let's thank God for that forgiveness. If you feel like you don't have very many friends because you've been mean to them, ask Jesus to forgive you and then ask your friends to forgive you. And ask God to forgive you for the other wrong things you've done.

Have the children spend time in prayer. Say: God says that he forgives us when we ask him to. You are completely forgiven for your sins—God doesn't remember them anymore. Isn't that wonderful! On the count of three, let's yell, "Thank you, God!" as loud as we can. Ready? One…two…three…Thank you, God!

Craft Corner

Give each child a two-sided photocopy of the "Zacchaeus" Collect-a-Craft handout (pp. 81-82). Have them color their take-home papers. Help them cut out the Jesus and Zacchaeus figures. Then help children fold and staple their Bibleramas in place (see page 6). Give children each a twig cut from a tree, and have them glue it to the left side of the Biblerama. Use one of the Bibleramas with the figures to tell the story to the children again. Remember to emphasize that Jesus forgave Zacchaeus.

Have preschoolers form pairs. Direct children to use their Bibleramas to tell each other the Bible story.

Listen in as pairs tell the story and help them with details they miss or misunderstand. Encourage children to use their Bibleramas to tell the story of Zacchaeus to their parents.

Let's Eat!

Have the children wash their hands. Set out vanilla wafers and tell children to pretend the snacks are the money that Zacchaeus collected from the people. Give the children some ready-made frosting to spread on the vanilla wafers. Each child should put several frosted cookies on a paper plate.

Remind children there were three steps in this forgiveness story:

1. Jesus gave forgiveness to Zacchaeus and to us.
2. Zacchaeus gave the money back to the people.
3. We can give forgiveness to our friends.

Ask children to hold their plates of cookies while forming a circle. Have the children pass their plates to those on their right to represent Jesus giving forgiveness to Zacchaeus. Have the children pass the plates to those next to them, representing Zacchaeus giving the money back. Then have the children pass the plates one more time, representing how they can forgive others. Then say: **We can eat our Forgiveness Snack together because we're all forgiven.**

Let's Sing!

Small or Tall

(Sing to the tune of "The Noble Duke of York.")

When you sing the word *small*, bend low; on the word *tall*, stand on tiptoe.

There was a man called Zacchaeus.

He wasn't very tall.

He wanted to see Jesus so he climbed up in a tree.

When you're tall, you're tall.

And when you're small, you're small.

And when you're only halfway up *(crouch halfway)*,

You're neither small nor tall.

When Zacchaeus had done wrong things,

He felt very small. *(Crouch down.)*

But when God forgave him,

He felt ten feet tall. *(Stand up tall.)*

When you're small, you're small. *(Crouch down.)*

And when you're tall, you're tall. *(Stand up tall.)*

And when you're only halfway up *(crouch halfway)*,

You're neither small nor tall.

Forgive, Forgive

(Sing to the tune of "Rejoice in the Lord Always.")

Forgive as the Lord forga-ave you, Colossians 3:13.

Forgive as the Lord forga-ave you, Colossians 3:13.

Forgive, forgive, again I say forgive!

Forgive, forgive, again I say forgive!

Let's Pray!

Before class, cut some pretend coins out of paper. Ask children to gather nearby. Remind children that when Zacchaeus knew he was forgiven by God he gave the money back to people he had taken it from. Give children a few of the pretend coins. Say: **These "coins" represent God's forgiveness. I gave them to you just like God gives his forgiveness. It's a free gift.** Ask one of the children to say a prayer thanking God for his forgiveness.

Our Key Verse from the Bible is Colossians 3:13. It says, "Forgive as the Lord forgave you." So I want you to give a coin to someone else in the room and say, "God forgives us."

Close by holding hands in a circle and singing the following song to the tune of "Rejoice in the Lord Always."

Forgive, Forgive

Forgive as the Lord forga-ave you, Colossians 3:13.

Forgive as the Lord forga-ave you, Colossians 3:13.

Forgive, Forgive, again I say forgive!

Forgive, Forgive, again I say forgive!

No More Sin!

Bible Story

Jesus died for our sins (Luke 24:1-12, 46).

The Point

This lesson will help children understand that because he loves us, ★Jesus died for our sins.

Key Verse

"For God so loved the world that he gave his one and only Son" (John 3:16).

About This Lesson

In this lesson, preschoolers will realize that when Jesus died, he took away all the bad things we've done.

Children will...

- talk about what it means to have sins taken away.
- work together to create a puzzle that tells about Jesus' death and resurrection.
- make reminders that Jesus died and rose again.

What You'll Need

- Bible
- two-sided photocopy of the "Jesus Died for Our Sins" Collect-a-Craft handout for each child (pp. 83-84)
- photocopy of the Bible Story Puzzle (p. 40)
- safety scissors
- stapler
- modeling dough
- plastic knives
- one pair of adult scissors
- clear tape
- pretzel sticks
- napkins
- crayons
- glue
- baby wipes

Bible Background for Teacher Enrichment

Jesus' ministry on earth was amazing. A carpenter who claimed to be the Son of God definitely caused a stir in the neighborhood! But Jesus did more than get people talking. He healed lame legs...and broken hearts. He filled baskets with fish and bread...and lives with purpose and hope. And this eye-popping, heart-stopping exhibition of God's love didn't stop when Jesus died—why, that was just the beginning! Jesus' death and resurrection were the ultimate example of God's love for humanity.

Preschoolers have a basic understanding of the concept of love. They love everything from the dog to strawberry ice cream! Yet, you can start helping

---

Preschool Pointer

You may be hesitant to talk about something as serious as death with the preschoolers in your class. But it's important for children to gain a simple understanding that all things die...even you and I! What better way to introduce them to the truth that we can have eternal life because of Jesus!

children develop a more accurate understanding of love by introducing them to the incredible love Jesus has for us. Use this lesson to help children realize that Jesus' love is bigger and better than anything else.

Welcome!

Gather children around a table, and give each child a handful of modeling dough. Let children roll out their dough so it's nice and smooth. Then let them use plastic knives to make marks on it.

Ask: • **How can you get rid of the marks on your dough?**

Say: **To make your dough smooth again, you need to start over and roll out the dough. Sometimes we have "marks" or wrong things that we do in real life.** Let children name some of the wrong things they do, such as lying, saying unkind words, or disobeying.

Ask: • **How can you get rid of those bad things?**

Say: **Because he loves us so much, ⭐ Jesus died for our sins. Jesus wants to take away all those bad things we do. Today we'll learn what God's Son, Jesus, did to take away our sins.**

Bible Story Fun

Before class, photocopy the Bible Story Puzzle (p. 40), then cut apart the puzzle pieces and hide them in your classroom.

Form a circle and say: **Clues about our Bible story are hidden around our room. Will you help me find them? Look for the puzzle piece clues in the classroom. If you find one, come back and sit with me.** When all the pieces are found, bring everyone back together in a circle. Open your Bible to Luke 24, and show the children the words.

Let's find out what happens in this amazing Bible story. This story is sort of a puzzle—lots of sad and strange things happen. Who has the piece with a mad face on it? Let the child with the piece set it in the middle of the circle. **Jesus is God's Son. A long time ago, he taught people about God. He showed God's love and power by healing people. That made most people very happy! But it made some people mad. They didn't believe that Jesus was God's Son. So they had him arrested.**

Ask for the puzzle piece with a picture of a cross on it. Place the puzzle piece in the middle of the circle, taping it to the previous one. Say: **Soldiers nailed Jesus to a cross like this one. That hurt Jesus. He hung on the cross until he died.** Ask for the puzzle piece with a picture of a sad face on it. Place the piece in the middle of the circle, taping it to the others. **That was a sad day for Jesus' friends. Ask for the puzzle piece with a picture of a tomb on it.** Place the piece in the middle of the circle, taping it to the others. **Jesus' friends took his body and placed it in a tomb—**

Teacher Tip

You may want to mount the puzzle pieces on poster board cut to size to make a sturdier puzzle.

kind of like a big cave. They rolled a giant rock over the entrance so no one could touch Jesus' body.

Ask for the puzzle piece with a picture of a "3" on it. Place the piece in the middle of the circle, taping it to the others. Say: **After three days, Jesus' friends came to put sweet-smelling spices on his body. But they were in for a surprise!** Ask for the puzzle piece with a picture of Jesus on it. Place the piece in the middle of the circle, taping it to the others. **Jesus was alive! He was stronger than death. Jesus died to take away all the bad things we do.** Point to the heart-shaped puzzle. **Because he loves us so much,** ⭐ **Jesus died for our sins.**

Open your Bible to John 3:16, and show the children the verse.

Say: **Listen to what the Bible says in John 3:16. The Bible says, "For God so loved the world that he gave his one and only Son." That means God loves us so much that he sent Jesus. When we believe in Jesus, we can live forever with God! Let's make something to remind us that** ⭐ **Jesus died for our sins.**

Craft Corner

Give each child a two-sided photocopy of the "Jesus Died for Our Sins" handout (pp. 83-84). Let children color their take-home papers. Then distribute safety scissors, and let children cut off the figures of Jesus and fold the figures on the dotted lines. Help children glue the figures together, back to back, making sure not to glue the tabs together. Show the children how to bend the tabs near Jesus' feet so the figure stands up. Help children fold and staple their Bibleramas in place. (Complete instructions can be found on page 6.) Then help children glue the Jesus figure to the floor of the scene.

Say: **When Jesus' friends went to the tomb, they never expected to discover that Jesus was alive! Jesus died and rose again because he loves us.** ⭐ **Jesus died for our sins.**

When you get home you can use your craft to tell your family that because he loves us, ⭐ **Jesus died for our sins. But right now, let's set our crafts aside so we can enjoy a snack!**

Have the children set their crafts aside until the close of the lesson.

Let's Eat!

Have the children wash their hands before snack time. Give each child a handful of pretzel sticks and a napkin. Say: **Let's use these pretzels to remember our Bible story. Can you use your pretzels to make a heart shape?** Let children make pretzel hearts on their napkins. **That reminds us that Jesus loves us. Remember how we couldn't get rid of the marks on the modeling clay in the beginning of class? That's what it's like with our sins—we can't get rid of them by ourselves. But**

For Extra Fun

Let children glue scraps of sandpaper to the tomb to add texture to the craft.

Allergy Alert

Be aware that some children have food allergies that can be dangerous. Know your children, and consult with parents about allergies their children may have. Also be sure to carefully read food labels, as hidden ingredients can cause allergy-related problems.

⭐Jesus died for our sins. Can you make a cross with your pretzels? Let children make pretzel crosses. That reminds us that Jesus died on the cross so we can be forgiven for our sins. Can you make a happy face with your pretzels? Let children make smiley faces with their pretzels. That reminds us that we can be glad because Jesus died on the cross and rose again so he could take away all the wrong things we do! Let's pray and thank God for his love and for this yummy snack!

Lead children in a simple prayer. Then let them enjoy their pretzels.

Teacher Tip

Have children wash their hands before snack time. If you don't have access to water, keep a supply of wet wipes for children to use.

Let's Sing!

After children finish their snack, let them help you clean up. Then teach children the following songs and motions to help them remember that ⭐Jesus died for our sins.

Do You Know?

(Sing to the tune of "The Muffin Man.")

Do you know that Jesus loves you *(point to a friend),*

Jesus loves you *(point to a different friend),*

Jesus loves you? *(Point to a different friend.)*

Do you know that Jesus loves you? *(Point to a different friend.)*

He'll take away your sins! *(Raise hands and wiggle fingers.)*

Jesus Died

(Sing to the tune of "Twinkle, Twinkle Little Star.")

Do you know why Jesus died? *(Shrug shoulders.)*

On a cross he gave his life. *(Stretch arms out to side.)*

Jesus is God's only Son. *(Point up.)*

He forgives us, everyone. *(Point to others in class.)*

Do you know why Jesus died? *(Shrug shoulders.)*

Jesus loves us—that is why! *(Hug self.)*

Let's Pray!

Gather children in a circle. Say: Because he loves us so much, ⭐Jesus died for our sins. When Jesus died and rose again, he made it possible for us to be forgiven for all the wrong things we do. Those bad things are called sins. Let's pray and thank Jesus for taking away our sins.

Distribute baby wipes, and have the children silently wipe their hands as you pray: Dear Jesus, thank you for loving us. Thank you for washing away our sins by dying on the cross for us. We love you. In Jesus' name, amen.

Let children drop their wipes in a trash can as they say, "Jesus loves me!"

Bible Story Puzzle

Made With Love

Bible Story

God creates the world (Genesis 1:1-31).

The Point

This lesson will help children understand that because he loves us,
⭐ **God made us.**

Key Verse

"God saw all that he had made, and it was very good" (Genesis 1:31a).

About This Lesson

Use this lesson to begin to teach preschoolers that God values them because he made them. Preschoolers can learn that God made them with lots of love.

Children will...

- make potato people.
- hear a rhyme about creation and bring their potato people "into" the world.
- create a craft that shows a creation scene.
- make a "creation" snack.

What You'll Need

- Bible
- washed and dried potato for each child
- markers
- two-sided photocopy of the "Creation" Collect-a-Craft handout for each child (pp. 85-86)
- stapler
- safety scissors
- glue sticks or glue
- modeling clay
- animal crackers
- fish-shaped crackers
- people-shaped cookies
- blueberry yogurt
- green food coloring
- shredded coconut
- crayons
- paper plates and napkins
- plastic spoons

Preschool Pointer

Transition times can be difficult for young children. Help your lesson flow smoothly by giving children a two-minute warning when you're wrapping up an activity. Also be sure to use the same attention-getting signal consistently. You might want to use a fun whistle or a special song to transition from one part of the lesson to another. (If you decide to flip the lights as a signal, be sure no one in your class suffers from seizures, as in some cases, blinking lights can be a trigger.)

Bible Background for Teacher Enrichment

The story of God's creation of the universe is central to Christianity. The human race was no accident and certainly not some cosmic unwanted child. As the chapter unfolds, it becomes apparent that humanity is that pinnacle of creation. After creating humanity, God even gave people a special place as the stewards over the rest of creation.

Preschoolers can understand that God made them with a lot of love and care. And they can begin to understand that they are valuable to God because they are his crowning creation. Use this lesson as a way of introducing God's incredible love for those he created!

Welcome!

Before class, wash and dry the potatoes. Set the potatoes and markers in the center of a table. Have the children sit around the table.

Say: **Let's make potato people! Draw two eyes, a nose, and a mouth on your potato.** Give the children a few minutes to draw facial features on their potatoes.

When everyone has finished, go around the table and let each child introduce his or her potato person to the rest of the class.

Ask: • **How did you decide which face parts to put on your potato person?**

• **How did it feel to make a potato person?**

• **What do you think it would be like to make *real* people?**

Say: **It felt good to create a potato person, didn't it? You got to make your person just the way you wanted. Today we're going to learn that because he loves us, ★ God made *us*! We'll also learn how God feels about all the people he made. Let's get started!**

Have the children set aside their potato people for use later in the lesson.

Bible Story Fun

For Extra Fun

Let children use crayons and markers to color in the facial features before they glue them on their potatoes. You could also provide fabric scraps for children to glue on as clothes.

Give each child a small ball of modeling clay.

Say: **I'm going to read a fun rhyme about how God made the world in six days. After I tell you what God did on each day, you can make something with your clay about God's creation. Ready? Let's start!**

Read the children the following rhyme. Pause after each day's rhyme to let children use their clay to depict that day's creation.

Say: **Day one, day one,**

God did all right!

God made the morning

And the night.

Have the children form models from their clay to remind them of how God made the day and night. Let children show off their creations to one another before moving on.

Say: **Day two, day two,**

God's not through.

He made the sky

For me and you!

Have the children form models from their clay to remind them of how God made the sky. Let children show off their creations to one another before moving on.

Say: **Day three, day three,**

What can it be?

God made the land

And plants and seas!

Have the children form models from their clay to remind them of how God made the land, plants, and seas. Let children show off their creations to one another before moving on.

Say: **Day four, day four,**

God's back for more.

The sun for the day

And the moon while we snore.

Have the children form models from their clay to remind them of how God made the sun and moon. Let children show off their creations to one another before moving on.

Say: **Day five, day five,**

What's next to arrive?

God made birds that fly

And fish that dive!

Have the children form models from their clay to remind them of how God made the birds and fish. Let children show off their creations to one another before moving on.

Say: **Day six, day six,**

God's favorite picks.

When God made people,

Love was in his mix.

Have the children form models from their clay to remind them of how God made people. Let children show off their creations to one another before moving on.

Collect the modeling clay for use later in the lesson. Have the children retrieve the potato people they made in the "Welcome!" activity, and pretend to bring them into the world that God created by bringing them back to the circle.

Ask: **• How do you think your potato people would feel to be brought into the wonderful world we just rhymed about?**

Say: **The Bible tells us that the first people God made were named Adam and Eve.**

Ask: **• How do you think Adam and Eve felt when they saw the wonderful world God had created for them?**

Say: **God make everything in the world—the water, the mountains, the animals, and the people. That means that God made you and me!**

Ask: **• How do you feel knowing that God made you?**

• What do you think of the world that God made for us?

• Why do you think God made the world and you and me?

Say: Because God loves us, ⭐ God made us. He made us with lots of care and love. And God made each one of us different and special—just like you all made your potato people different. And do you know what else? God said that everything he made was good! Open your Bible to Genesis 1:31a, and show the children the verse. Listen while I read our Key Verse: "God saw all that he had made, and it was very good." ⭐ God made us and loves us very much! Let's make something to help us remember that because he loves us, ⭐ God made us.

Have the children set aside their potato people.

Craft Corner

Give each child a two-sided photocopy of the "Creation" Collect-a-Craft handout (pp. 85-86). Let children color their craft papers. Distribute safety scissors and glue sticks. Let children cut out the animal and people figures from the bottom of the page. Then help children fold and staple their Bibleramas into place. (Complete instructions can be found on page 6.) Show the children how to fold the tabs on the bottom of the figures and glue them inside the scene.

Say: When you get home you can use your craft to tell your family how ⭐ God made us. Right now, though, let's set our crafts aside so we can enjoy a fun snack!

Let's Eat!

Before class, use green food coloring to tint coconut to make "grass."

Have children wash their hands. Give each child a paper plate, and show the children how to sprinkle the coconut grass on their plates. Let them spoon a little blueberry yogurt onto their plates to make an "ocean." Let children add fish-shaped crackers to the ocean and animal cracker "animals" to the scene. Finally, let each child add two people-shaped cookies to the scene.

Say: Because he loves us, ⭐ God made us. And he made a wonderful world for us to live in. Before we eat our snacks, let's thank God for making us and our wonderful world.

Lead children in a short prayer of thanks. Then let them eat their snacks. As children are enjoying their treats, ask them to name their favorite parts of creation. After children finish eating, ask them to help clean up so they can sing some fun songs!

For Extra Fun

Provide fabric and construction paper scraps for children to glue to their scenes as clothing and grass. You could even provide small twigs and leaves for a more "realistic" garden.

Allergy Alert

Be aware that some children have food allergies that can be dangerous. Know your children, and consult with parents about allergies their children may have. Also be sure to carefully read food labels, as hidden ingredients can cause allergy-related problems.

Teacher Tip

If you don't have access to water, keep a supply of baby wipes for children to use.

Let's Sing!

Teach children the following songs and motions to help them remember that because he loves us, ⭐ God made us.

God Made You and Me!

(Sing to the tune of "If You're Happy and You Know It.")

Because he loves us, God made you and me. *(Clap, clap.)*

Because he loves us, God made you and me. *(Clap, clap.)*

God made us all with care. *(Stretch arms over head.)*

That proves his love is there. *(Cross arms over chest.)*

Because he loves us, God made you and me. *(Clap, clap.)*

God Made It All

(Sing to the tune of "Jesus Loves Me.")

God made you *(point to another person)*,

And God made me. *(Point to self.)*

He made the donkey *(pretend to ride)*

And the tree. *(Stretch out arms.)*

He made the tiger *(pretend to claw in air)*

And the rest. *(Stretch arms out wide.)*

But he made people *(point to others)*

The very best. *(Clap hands.)*

Yes, God made you. *(Point to another person.)*

Yes, God made me. *(Point to self.)*

Yes, God made us. *(Point to others.)*

He made us with his love. *(Cross arms over chest.)*

Let's Pray!

Have the children sit in a circle on the floor. Give each child a ball of modeling clay from earlier in the lesson. Instruct the children to shape the clay into a model of themselves. Explain that as you pray, each child will set his or her clay figure in the center of the circle.

Pray: **Dear God, thank you for making us. Thank you for making each one of us special. Thank you for** [go around the circle and name each child, letting children each place their clay figures in the circle]. **Thank you for loving us. In Jesus' name, amen.**

Collect the clay, and remind children to take home their Bibleramas and potato people.

God's Rules Rule!

Bible Story

God gives us the Ten Commandments (Exodus 20:1-17).

The Point

This lesson will help preschoolers understand that ⭐ **God teaches us.**

Key Verse

"These commandments that I give you today are to be upon your hearts" (Deuteronomy 6:6).

About This Lesson

Use this fun lesson to show the children that because God loves us, he wants us to learn his special rules.

Children will...

• learn how to make paper hearts.

• use an action rhyme to learn the Ten Commandments.

• pray and ask God to help them obey his important rules.

What You'll Need

• Bible
• two-sided photocopy of the "Ten Command-ments" Collect-a-Craft handout for each child (pp. 87-88)
• stapler
• crayons
• construction paper

• marker
• safety scissors
• glue sticks or glue
• flour tortillas
• small bowls of frosting
• plastic knives
• heart-shaped cookie cutters
• paper plates and napkins

Bible Background for Teacher Enrichment

You might say that the Israelites had front row seats at countless displays of God's amazing power. God's people listened as the Egyptians wept over lost sons. They ran ahead when God parted the waters of the Red Sea. They tasted sweet manna and gulped fresh water that God had provided. And they defeated the Amalekites with God's miraculous power. God had certainly revealed his power—now it was time to reveal his plan. "Now if you obey me fully...then out of all nations you will be my treasured possession" (Exodus 19:5). Through the Ten Commandments, God laid out a set of rules that would guide his people morally and spiritually.

The preschoolers in your class are learning that rules can be helpful and

Preschool Pointer

Keep your classroom rules short, sweet, and general so children can easily remember them. Phrases like "Be kind," "Be safe," or "Be a friend" are friendly and appropriate for preschoolers. Briefly review your rules at the start of each class time so everyone has the benefit of knowing what is and isn't acceptable.

good. They're realizing that rules are there to keep us safe and help us get along with each other. So this is a wonderful time to expose children to God's rules—the most important ones of all! The activities in this lesson will guide children to discover that God gave us rules because he loves us and wants us to know how to follow him.

Welcome!

Before children arrive, fold sheets of construction paper in half. You'll need one sheet for every child in class. Use a marker to draw half of a heart shape along the folded edge. Then unfold the papers and set them aside.

When everyone has arrived, gather children around a table.

Say: **I'm so glad to see you all here today! I have something fun to teach you. Watch what I do, then you'll have a turn!**

Fold a sheet of construction paper in half, and draw half of a heart shape along the folded edge. Keep the paper folded, and cut along the line. Open the paper, and show the children the completed heart.

Say: **That's an easy way to make a pretty heart, isn't it? Now it's your turn to try.**

Distribute the folded papers you prepared ahead of time, and guide children in cutting their papers. (You may need to remind some children of the correct way to hold scissors.) Help children write their names on their paper hearts, then collect the hearts and scissors.

Ask: • **What did I teach you to do?**

• **Who else teaches you how to do things?**

• **What do they teach you?**

Say: **Today we're going to learn that** ★ **God teaches us, too.** Hold up a Bible. **God gave us the Bible—it's his Word. The Bible is filled with important things God wants us to learn.**

Ask: • **Why do you think God wants to teach us?**

• **How can learning God's rules help us?**

Say: **Today we'll learn about ten important rules that God taught to his people long ago. God loved those people and wanted them to live the right way. And God loves** *us* **and wants us to live the right way too! Let's learn more about God's important rules!**

Bible Story Fun

Open your Bible to Exodus 20, and show the children the words.

Say: **The Bible tells us of the wonderful things God did for his special people. He saved them from a wicked king. He fed them special food from heaven. God even made water come from a rock so his people wouldn't be thirsty! God loved his**

Teacher Tip

Younger preschoolers are still mastering the fine motor skills needed to use scissors, so this activity is great practice for them! Help children be successful by providing them with child-safe scissors and by making dark marker lines that are easy for them to see and follow.

people, and he wanted them to live the right way. He wanted them to be safe and happy. So God taught his people ten special rules called commandments. Let's learn what they are!

Lead children in the following action rhyme. Be sure to go through the rhyme slowly so children can follow along.

Don't worship any gods, but me—*(shake your head "no")*.

I am the one true God, you see! *(Point up.)*

Don't make a statue. Don't bow down low. *(Pound your fists together.)*

I am the only God, don't you know! *(Point up.)*

Treat my name in a special way *(cup hands around mouth)*

While you work and rest and play. *(March in place.)*

Remember the Sabbath—be sure to rest! *(Rest head on hands.)*

That's a special day that's blessed.

Be sure to obey your mom and dad. *(Stretch out right arm on "mom" and left arm on "dad," as if hugging them.)*

That will surely make me glad! *(Move arms in to hug yourself.)*

Never hurt or kill another—*(shake head "no")*

That means you must be kind to each other. *(Pat someone on the back.)*

Keep your promise to your husband or wife. *(Pretend to put on a wedding ring.)*

Be faithful to them for all of your life. *(Stretch out arms on "all.")*

Do not take your neighbors things *(pull arms to chest, as if holding something)*—

That's called stealing, not borrowing! *(Hold arms out to someone, as if giving.)*

Do not ever tell a lie. *(Shake head "no.")*

Only speak words that are true and right. *(Raise one hand on "true" and one on "right.")*

Be happy with all I've given you. *(Stretch out arms on "all.")*

Don't wish for things your friends have, too.

Lead children in the rhyme and motions several more times to help them learn the Ten Commandments. Then ask:

• Why did God want people to learn the Ten Commandments?

• What are some other ways that God shows us his love?

Say: God gave ten special rules that would help his people live good, safe, happy lives. ★ God teaches us, too. God knows that his rules are good and will keep us safe and happy. When we obey God's rules, we'll be happy and God will be happy too! Let's make something to help us remember God's Ten Commandments.

Craft Corner

Say: ★ God teaches us because he loves us. He wants us to learn his special rules called the Ten Commandments. Open your Bible to the Key Verse, Deuteronomy

6:6, and show the children the verse. **Listen to what the Bible says about God's commandments: "These commandments that I give you today are to be upon your hearts."** That means God wants us to remember all the things he teaches us! Let's put some of God's commandments on these hearts.

Give each child a two-sided photocopy of the "Ten Commandments" Collect-a-Craft handout (pp. 87-88). Let children color their craft papers. Distribute safety scissors and glue. Let children cut out the "commandments" from the bottom of the page and glue them to the hearts in the background. Then help children fold and staple their Bibleramas into place. (Complete instructions can be found on page 6.)

Say: **When you get home you can use your craft to tell your family all about God's Ten Commandments! But for now, let's set the crafts aside so we can enjoy a yummy snack!**

Have the children set their crafts aside until the close of the lesson.

Let's Eat!

Have the children wash their hands. Set out small flour tortillas, plastic knives, small bowls of frosting, and heart-shaped cookie cutters. Read aloud the Key Verse, Deuteronomy 6:6: **"These commandments that I give you today are to be upon your hearts."** Let children cut heart shapes from the tortillas and then "write" some of God's rules on their hearts with the frosting. As children work, remind them that God wants us to obey his special rules because he loves us.

When everyone has finished making a snack, lead the children in a short prayer thanking God for the food. As children enjoy their snacks, ask them to think about why ⭐ God teaches us, and ask which of the Ten Commandments are their favorites. After children finish eating, ask them to help clean up so they can sing some fun songs!

Let's Sing!

Teach children the following songs and motions to help them remember that because he loves us, ⭐ God teaches us.

Ten Little Rules

(Sing to the tune of "Ten Little Indians.")

Have the children hold up the right number of fingers as they count with this song.

One rule, two rules, three rules from God.

Four rules, five rules, six rules from God.

Seven rules, eight rules, nine rules from God.

Ten rules that ⭐ God teaches us!

For Extra Fun

Let children create paper people to stand inside their crafts. Give each child a small oval piece of paper, and let children draw themselves and family members. Then let children bend the tabs on the bottom of the figures and glue them to the floor of their crafts.

Allergy Alert

Be aware that some children have food allergies that can be dangerous. Know your children, and consult with parents about allergies their children may have. Also be sure to carefully read food labels, as hidden ingredients can cause allergy-related problems.

Teacher Tip

If you don't have access to water, keep a supply of baby wipes for children to use.

God Teaches Me

(Sing to the tune of "Bingo.")

God gave ten important rules *(hold up ten fingers)*

To help us do the right things. *(Nod head.)*

Yes, God teaches me! *(Point to self.)*

Yes, God teaches you! *(Point to a friend.)*

Yes, God teaches us! *(Pat two friends on back.)*

And we'll do what God tells us. *(Nod head.)*

Let's Pray!

Use the paper hearts from the "Welcome!" activity to form a short path of hearts. (It's a good idea to tape the hearts to the floor.) Gather children at one end of the path.

Say: **God teaches us because he loves us. God is happy when we follow his rules. Let's pray and ask God to help us obey his rules and keep them close to our hearts.**

Let children take turns walking along the path. As children walk, have them pray, "Dear God, help me to obey your rules." Gather children in a circle at the other end, join hands and pray: **In Jesus' name, amen.**

God's a Good Listener

Bible Story

God hears Hannah's prayer (1 Samuel 1:1-20).

The Point

This lesson will teach children that because he loves us,  **God listens to our prayers.**

Key Verse

"He answered their prayers, because they trusted in him" (1 Chronicles 5:20b).

About This Lesson

In this lesson, preschoolers will learn that God loves them so much that he will always listen to them.

Children will...

- discover that God listens to them any time of the day.
- learn how God listened and helped a woman named Hannah.
- create a yummy treat that reminds them that God is listening around the clock.

What You'll Need

- Bible
- two-sided photocopy of the "Hannah" Collect-a-Craft handout for each child (pp. 89-90)
- clock with movable hands (or paper-plate "clock" with paper hands)
- baby doll
- stapler
- glue sticks
- safety scissors
- crayons
- round crackers
- soft cream cheese
- pretzel sticks
- plastic knives
- paper plates and napkins

Bible Background for Teacher Enrichment

The story of Hannah takes place during the times of the judges. During those days women were considered failures when they could not conceive children. But Hannah's inability to have a baby was part of God's excellent plan. Hannah prayed to God, pleading for a baby. God listened and answered her prayer. Hannah's son, Samuel, would go on to become an exemplary example of what a judge should be.

Use this lesson to teach preschoolers that God will always hear us when we

Preschool Pointer

Preschoolers are accustomed to having their requests responded to in a timely manner. At this age they don't have a great deal of patience. That's why the story of Hannah is so important for them to learn. God was aware of Hannah's deep desire for a child. God heard her prayers and responded when the time was right. God granted her a very special child that she devoted to God's service. Preschoolers need to understand that just because they want something, doesn't mean God will immediately produce it. Instead, God will always hear our prayers, and he will respond in whatever way and time is best for us. Emphasize to children that because God loves us so much, we can trust that he knows what is best.

pray to him. Also stress that God responds to our prayers in his own time so that whatever happens will ultimately be best for us and for his kingdom. As you teach children how God answered Hannah's prayer, you'll be helping them build a framework of trust in God that will them the rest of their lives!

Welcome!

Greet children each by name as they arrive and welcome them to your class. Gather children together in the center of the room, and show them the clock with movable hands. Point the hands to 12:00.

Ask: • **What are you usually doing at 12 o'clock noon each day?**

• **Do you think God would hear you if you prayed at noon? Why do you think that?**

Move the hands to 1:00, and repeat the questions. Then let each child take a turn moving the hands of the clock to a new time. You'll probably need to help children read the result and describe the time of day they selected. For example, "OK, 3:20 is in the afternoon. What are some things you do in the afternoon? Would God hear you if you prayed at 3:20?"

Say: **No matter what time of the day or night,** ⭐ **God listens to our prayers. In today's Bible story, we'll meet a woman named Hannah. Hannah trusted God to answer her prayer. You know, that's just what the Bible says to do.** Open your Bible to 1 Chronicles 5:20b, and show the children the verse. **Listen while I read our Key Verse, 1 Chronicles 5:20b: "He answered their prayers, because they trusted in him."** Have the children repeat the verse with you several times. **In today's Bible story, Hannah prayed to God for something special, and God heard her prayer. Let's find out what she prayed for!**

Bible Story Fun

Have the children sit in a circle. Open your Bible to 1 Samuel 1:1-20, and show the children the passage.

Say: **Today's Bible story comes from 1 Samuel 1:1-20. The story is about a woman named Hannah. Hannah wanted very much to have a baby.** Hold up the baby doll.

Ask • **What sound do babies make a lot?**

Say: **That's right! Babies cry a lot. They go, "Waa! Waa!" Let's practice that.** Lead kids in pretending to cry like babies. **As I tell today's story, I want you to make that crying sound every time you hear me say the word** *baby*. **We'll pass this baby doll around the circle, and every time you hear me say** *baby*, **we'll all pretend to cry, and the person holding the doll at the time can pretend to rock the baby.**

Make sure children understand the instructions. Then read the following rhyme, pausing every time you say *baby*. Prompt children in the responses you explained.

> A woman named Hannah,
> She prayed and she prayed.
> She wanted a baby
> To hold every day.
>
> She waited and waited,
> And it made her so sad,
> To wish for a baby
> Like other women had.
>
> The others, you see,
> Were quite nasty and wry.
> They made fun of Hannah,
> Even making her cry.
>
> Hannah cried to the Lord,
> And he heard from above.
> God gave her a baby
> To show her his love.
>
> A woman named Hannah,
> She prayed and she prayed.
> God gave her a baby
> To hold every day.

Repeat the rhyme several times to give every child a chance to rock the baby doll.

Ask: • Why was Hannah so sad in the beginning of this story?

• What did Hannah do when she was so sad?

• What did God do when Hannah prayed?

Say: God listened to Hannah's prayers and gave her a baby. And do you know what? ⭐ God listens to our prayers, too! No matter where we are or what we're doing, God *always* hears our prayers. Let's make something to help us remember that ⭐ God listens to our prayers.

Craft Corner

Give each child a two-sided photocopy of the "Hannah" Collect-a-Craft handout (pp. 89-90). Let children color their craft papers. Distribute safety scissors and glue. Let children cut out the Hannah and baby figure from the bottom

For Extra Fun

Provide small fabric scrap "blankets" for children to glue to the baby figure in the scene.

Allergy Alert

Be aware that some children have food allergies that can be dangerous. Know your children, and consult with parents about allergies their children may have. Also be sure to carefully read food labels, as hidden ingredients can cause allergy-related problems.

Teacher Tip

If you don't have access to water, keep a supply of baby wipes for children to use.

of the page. Then help children fold and staple their Bibleramas into place. (Complete instructions can be found on page 6.) Show the children how to fold the tabs on the bottom of the figures they cut out, and glue the figures inside the scene. Have the children glue the baby figure in the picture of the cradle.

Say: **When you get home you can use your craft to tell your family all about how God listened to Hannah's prayers and ⭐ God listens to our prayers. But right now, let's set the crafts aside so we can enjoy a yummy snack!**

Have the children set their crafts aside until the close of the lesson.

Let's Eat!

Have the children wash their hands before the snack. Explain to them that they'll be creating cookie clocks to remind them that ⭐ God listens to our prayers, no matter what time we pray!

Set out round crackers, soft cream cheese, thin pretzel sticks, plastic knives, napkins, and small paper plates. Let children each spread a few crackers with cream cheese to make clock faces. Then let children use pretzel stick pieces to create the hands of the clocks. As children hold up their clocks, tell each child what time the clock says and remind everyone that God hears our prayers at all times of the day!

Then let children enjoy their snacks. As children eat, ask them to think about why ⭐ God listens to our prayers. Invite children to share times God has listened to their prayers or the prayers of their families. After children finish eating, ask them to help clean up so they can sing some fun songs!

Let's Sing!

Teach children the following songs and motions to help them remember that ⭐ God listens to our prayers.

God Is Listening

(Sing to the tune of "Twinkle, Twinkle, Little Star.")

God is listening to your prayer. *(Put hand beside ear, then make praying hands.)*
God loves you and always cares. *(Point to others, then cross arms over chest.)*
It doesn't matter where you are *(spread arms to side),*
God loves you both near and far. *(Cross arms over chest.)*
God is listening to your prayer. *(Put hand beside ear, then make praying hands.)*
God loves you and always cares. *(Point to others, then cross arms over chest.)*

Talk to God!

(Sing to the tune of "Amen.")

Talk to God! Talk to God! Talk to God, to God, to God! *(Put hands beside mouth.)*

God hears us! God hears us! God hears us, hears us, hears us! *(Put hands beside ears.)*

God loves us! God loves us! God loves us, loves us, loves us! *(Put hands across chest.)*

Let's Pray!

Gather children in a circle. Teach them the following rhyme. Then lead children in praying for each other. Let each child take a turn standing in the center of a prayer circle while his or her name is inserted into the prayer.

God loves [child's name] **and listens to her** [his] **prayers.**

He listens to what she [he] **says and always shows he cares!**

After everyone has been prayed for in the center of the circle, have the children stand and hold hands. Close the prayer by thanking God for loving us and always listening to our prayers.

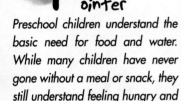

Preschool Pointer

Preschool children understand the basic need for food and water. While many children have never gone without a meal or snack, they still understand feeling hungry and the need to eat. Use this Bible story to help children understand that it is God who takes care of them and meets their basic needs.

Bible Story

God takes care of Elijah (1 Kings 17:1-6).

The Point

This lesson will help children understand that because he loves us, **God takes care of us.**

Key Verse

"The Lord watches over you" (Psalm 121:5a).

About This Lesson

Use this lesson to help children experience and understand that God loves us and takes cares of us.

Children Will...

- play a game acting out God's care of Elijah.
- sing a new song about God's care.
- learn how God cares for us.

What You'll Need

- Bible
- two-sided photocopy of the "Elijah" Collect-a-Craft handout for each child (pp. 91-92)
- bubbles
- safety scissors
- stapler
- glue sticks
- blue crepe paper
- croutons or bread
- blue Kool-Aid dry mix
- cups
- spoons
- pitchers of water
- pita bread cut into quarters
- lunch meat
- sliced cheese
- crumpled paper
- magazine pictures of food

Bible Background for Teacher Enrichment

When Solomon was King, Israel was on top of the world. Maybe the Israelites started to trust in the stuff God gave them instead of trusting in the one who gave them the stuff. Whatever happened, the people fell further away from God with each new king who came on the scene. And King Ahab was one of the worst. Ahab began worshipping the false god Baal and led the people in his evil ways.

God never stopped loving his people, but he had to do something to save them from their own sin. So God sent Elijah to talk to Ahab. Elijah told Ahab that no rain would fall on Israel until they got their priorities straight. The drought came quickly, just as Elijah said it would.

While everyone who turned away from God had their empty stomachs and thirsty mouths to remind them of their need for God, Elijah's needs were met. Every morning and every evening, God sent ravens to bring bread and meat to feed the obedient prophet. Elijah even drank from a brook that God showed him.

The preschoolers in your class may never know what it means to be in need. How important it is that they understand that God has provided for them. Help your preschoolers to see that the food and provision they experience is not a right. Rather, it is a wonderful gift from God that they can share with others.

Welcome!

Ask: • What's your favorite thing to eat?

• Have you ever been really, really hungry?

• What did you do?

Say: **Today we're going to learn about a man named Elijah who was really hungry. Elijah couldn't go to the refrigerator or ask his mom for a snack. You'll never guess how God brought food to this man. Go ahead. Try to guess.** Wait for guesses.

God had birds bring food to Elijah! Every morning and every night, birds dropped bread and meat in front of the man. Let's see what it was like to be fed by birds.

Select one member of the class to be "Elijah" seated on a chair. Tell Elijah to call out either "I'm hungry for food" or "I'm thirsty." Tell the rest of the class to wave their arms and act like birds when Elijah says he's hungry and pretend to give him food. If he says he's thirsty, have them make their fingers ripple like the brook and pretend to give water to Elijah.

Let children take turns being Elijah.

Say: **God took care of Elijah, and** ⭐ **God takes care of us too.**

Ask: • **What do you think it would be like to be fed by birds?**

• **Can you think of some ways that God takes care of you?**

Help preschoolers think of ways that God takes care of them, such as providing good things through their parents, giving them warm homes, and giving them friends.

Bible Story Fun

Open your Bible to 1 Kings and show children the words.

Say: **Let's learn a little more about Elijah and how God took care of him. This story is found in the Bible in 1 Kings 17. Every time I say the name Elijah, whisper "Elijah" and then stick your tongue out and pant like you're thirsty. Let's practice this to make sure you're ready to help tell our Bible story. Ready? Elijah.**

A long time ago, there was a man named *Elijah.* **He was a man of God called a prophet.** *Elijah's* **job was to give messages from God to the people. Ahab was a**

wicked king who was trying to get people to worship a pretend god, instead of the true God.

Say in a big voice: God decided, "I will not send the rain unless the people worship me and not their pretend god."

Ask: • Why do we need rain?

• What happens when it doesn't rain for a long time?

Say: When God gave *Elijah* that message, he planned take care of him in a special way and told *Elijah* where he could find water. So *Elijah* walked for a long time to find the special brook. Let's stand up and pretend to walk to that brook. Lead children to another part of your room. *Elijah* cupped his hands, put his hands into the brook, and drank the water. Let's pretend to drink water from the brook. Lead children in kneeling down and pretending to get water out of a stream.

Elijah realized that he was also very hungry. Let's rub our bellies to show we're hungry.

Ask: • How do you know when you're hungry?

• Where do you get food to eat when you're hungry?

Say: *Elijah* was not near a house with a kitchen, and there weren't any stores or fast-food restaurants nearby.

Ask: • How do you think he was going to eat?

• How do you think God could take care of *Elijah's* hunger?

Say: God knew *Elijah* was hungry and took care of him in a very special way. Big black birds called ravens flew to *Elijah* and brought him bread and meat. Blow bubbles over the children. Pretend these bubbles are pieces of food dropped by the birds. Grab as many of the bubbles as you can. Blow bubbles as long as children show interest. God sent the ravens with food for *Elijah* every morning and every night. Lead children in sticking out their bellies and patting them as if they're full. So, God did what he said and took care of *Elijah*. Thank you, God, for taking care of Elijah and thank you for taking care of us, too.

Ask: • What are ways that God takes care of you every day?

• Who gives you food to eat?

Say: Let's pray and thank God for the many ways he watches over us and takes care of us.

Craft Corner

Give each child a two-sided photocopy of the "Elijah" Collect-a-Craft handout (pp. 91-92). Let children color the pictures. Distribute safety scissors and glue sticks. Help children cut out the Elijah and raven figures from the bottom of the page. Then help children fold and staple their Bibleramas into place. (Complete instructions can be found on page 6.) Help children each fold the tabs on the

Elijah figure and glue or tape them near the brook.

Say: **Elijah was so hungry and so thirsty. God took care of Elijah, just like** ⭐ **God takes care of us. God gave Elijah water from a little river.**

Set out blue crepe paper, and have the children glue pieces of the paper to the rippling brook. Have children push Elijah's head near the brook, pretending to drink and say, "Ahh. Thank you, God, for the nice cool drink."

Ask: • **Where will Elijah get his food?**

Help children glue the ravens to the walls of the scene. Then help children glue croutons or small pieces of bread on the ground near Elijah. Have children push Elijah's head near the food, pretending to eat and say, "Yum. Thank you, God, for this tasty bread."

Say: **Elijah was hungry and thirsty and God took care of Elijah.** ⭐ **God takes care of you, too!**

Let's Eat!

Have children wash their hands. Form two groups. Have the first group make the drink for everyone. Set out a few spoons, pitchers of water, and glasses with blue Kool-Aid dry mix in the bottom of each cup. Let children pour some water in cups for themselves and one other person to make rippling brook drinks. Be prepared for and expect a few spills.

Have the second group make snacks for themselves and one for another person. Divide pita bread into quarters. Give each child two pita bread quarters, two thin slices of lunch meat, and two slices of cheese. Show each child how to make a sandwich for themselves and one other person.

Help children find partners to share their snack and drink with. Remind children that they took care of each other the way ⭐ God takes care of us.

Let's Sing!

Say: **Today we're going to learn how God took care of Elijah and how** ⭐ **God takes care of us. Let's learn a song, and then we'll do the actions that go with it.**

Let's choose one person to be Elijah and have that person lie down in the middle of our circle. The rest of us will flap our wings and drop crumpled paper as pretend food to Elijah when we sing about the ravens. Then when we sing about the rippling brook, we'll wave our blue streamers over Elijah.

Did You Ever See a Raven?

(Sing to the tune of "Did You Ever See a Lassie?")

Have Elijah sit in the middle of the circle. Give each child a piece of the blue crepe paper and crumpled sheet of paper. Do the actions mentioned in the song.

Teacher Tip

If you have food stickers, suggest that the children place food stickers on the ground near Elijah.

Allergy Alert

Be aware that some children have food allergies that can be dangerous. Know your children, and consult with parents about allergies their children may have. Also be sure to carefully read food labels, as hidden ingredients can cause allergy-related problems.

Teacher Tip

Have children wash their hands before snack time. If you don't have access to water, keep a supply of wet wipes for children to use.

Did you ever see a raven, a raven, a raven?

Did you ever see a raven give someone food?

Flap your wings up and down, give food to Elijah.

The Lord cared for Elijah and he cares for us too.

Did you ever see a rippling brook, rippling brook, rippling brook?

Did you ever see a rippling brook with water to drink?

Let's wave our streamers way over Elijah.

The Lord cared for Elijah and he cares for us too.

God Sent the Ravens

(Sing to the tune of "I've Got the Joy, Joy, Joy, Joy.")

God sent the ravens, ravens, ravens, to care for Elijah, to care for Elijah, to care for Elijah. *(Move around flapping wings.)*

God sent the rippling brook, the rippling brook to care for Elijah.

God will take care of you! *(Move around waving arms like flowing water.)*

Oh, I'm so happy, so very happy that ★ God takes care of you, and you, and you. *(Turn around in circles with arms waving high during the "happy" words, then point to children during the "you" words.)*

Oh, I'm so happy, so very happy that God takes care of you and you. *(Arms outstretched.)*

Let's Pray!

Bring in magazine pictures of food. Lay the pictures on the floor the way the ravens laid the food on the ground for Elijah. Ask the children to choose one picture of food they like and bring it to the circle. Have the children pray and thank God for that food. Close by thanking God for watching over each one of us and for taking care of us.

A Lion's Share of Protection

Bible Story

God protects Daniel in the lions' den (Daniel 6:1-23).

The Point

This lesson will teach children that because he loves us, ★ **God protects us.**

Key Verse

"Do not fear, for I am with you" (Isaiah 41:10a).

About This Lesson

In this lesson, preschoolers will learn that God loves us so much that he can and will protect us.

Children will...

- learn a fun rhyme about God's love and protection.
- participate in a responsive story about God's protection.
- make a delicious treat that will remind them how God protected Daniel.
- sing a song of praise to God for his protection.

What You'll Need

- Bible
- two-sided photocopy of the "Daniel" Collect-a-Craft handout for each child (pp. 93-94)
- large slips of paper with children's names printed on them
- pen
- crayons
- safety scissors
- stapler
- glue sticks
- small heart stickers
- sugar cookies
- frosting
- string licorice
- small candies
- candy hearts
- plastic knives
- paper plates and napkins
- yarn

Preschool Pointer

Preschoolers are beginning to develop an awareness of those they can trust and those they can't. As a representative of the church, it's important for you to be someone your preschoolers can look to with confidence. Make every effort to follow through on promises you make to your class, and if for some reason, you have to renege on an agreement, be sure to explain why. Even more importantly, stress to children that even though people may let them down sometimes, God will always be completely trustworthy!

Bible Background for Teacher Enrichment

This Bible story takes place while Daniel is working as one of King Darius' top administrators. Daniel was a hard worker who served God faithfully. Unfortunately those characteristics often drew the criticism of Daniel's peers, who were jealous of him. Because Daniel's life was beyond reproach, his detractors could find no ammunition with which to degrade him to the king. So they decided to attack his beliefs instead. By playing off the king's weakness of pride, they convinced the king to put himself in the position of a god whom everyone must worship. Everyone, that is, but Daniel!

Daniel's response was to refuse to worship the king and to continue to worship and pray to the one true God. Daniel was thrown into the lions' den as punishment. But Daniel relied on God, faithfully trusting him in all things. The result was God's miraculous protection—keeping Daniel safe and closing the lions' mouths. Daniel knew that God's will would always be done and felt the peace of knowing that God would always be with him. Use this lesson to help preschoolers understand that God is always in control and can always protect them, just as he did Daniel!

Welcome!

Before class, write each child's name on a separate large slip of paper, then hide the papers around the room.

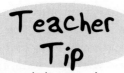

Teacher Tip

It's a good idea to jot down where you've hidden the papers in case you need to offer hints as children search.

After everyone has arrived, gather children together and ask them to raise their hands if they've ever been afraid. Pause to let them respond. Then tell children that you'll give them one minute to go around the room, shake hands with each person, and tell each person one thing they're afraid of. Give a starting signal, and let children mingle. Make sure to join in the activity yourself!

After a minute, call time and invite everyone together again.

Ask: • **What kinds of things are people in this room afraid of?**

• **What do you do when you're afraid?**

Say: **Sometimes when we're afraid, we try to run away or hide, like hiding under the covers during a thunderstorm. In our room, I've hidden slips of paper with your names on them. Let's see if we can find everyone's paper! But before we do, let's learn a new rhyme to say while we're looking for the papers.**

Teach children this simple rhyme:

God will protect me when I am afraid.

He loves me so much, he will come to my aid.

After children have learned the rhyme, let them hunt for the slips of paper. Explain that when each child finds a paper, he or she should give it to you and then sit in a circle on the floor. Lead children in repeating the rhyme together as they search. When everyone has given you a slip of paper and is sitting on the floor, continue.

Say: **God loves you so much, you don't have to run away or hide when you're afraid. Just as we brought these papers with your names out of hiding, we don't have to hide when we're afraid because** ⭐ **God protects us.** Open your Bible to Isaiah 41:10a, and show children the verse. **Listen to what today's Key Verse says: "So do not fear, for I am with you."** Have children repeat the verse with you several times.

Then give each child the paper slip with his or her name on it. Explain that you'll go around the circle and let each child place his or her paper slip in the center of the circle. As each child does so, lead the class in repeating the rhyme they learned earlier, personalizing the rhyme for each child. For example, you might say, "God will protect Jacob when he is afraid. He loves him so much, he will come to his aid."

After everyone has had the rhyme repeated for him or her, open your Bible. Show the children where the book of Isaiah is in the Old Testament.

Say: We've already learned that we don't have to be afraid because ⭐ God protects us. And do you know how I know that's true? Because the Bible says so! Listen as I read today's Key Verse from Isaiah 41:10a: "So do not fear, for I am with you." Have children repeat the verse with you several times. Today we're going to learn about a man who knew that God was with him, even though he faced some serious trouble. Let's find out more!

Bible Story Fun

Open your Bible to Daniel 6:1-23, and show children the passage.

Say: Today's Bible story comes from the book of Daniel. And since it's from the book of Daniel, it's not surprising that this story is about a man named Daniel. Daniel had a scary time when he was put into a den of hungry lions. Those lions wanted to eat Daniel, but God protected him. I'll tell you the story, but I'll need your help.

Explain that children will pretend to be lions as you tell the story. Designate an area of your room as the "lions' den." Have children crawl on all fours around the area and practice roaring like lions. After a few moments of roaring, explain that every time children hear the word lion during the story, they can roar and pretend to claw the air with their front "paws." Every time they hear the name Daniel they can rub their tummies and say, "Mmm, I'm hungry!" Have children practice the responses several times. Then read "Daniel's Tale" (p. 65) and prompt children to respond to the underlined words.

Craft Corner

Give each child a two-sided photocopy of the "Daniel" Collect-a-Craft handout (pp. 93-94). Set out crayons, safety scissors, and glue sticks for children to share. Let children color their craft papers. Then have children cut out the figures of Daniel and the lions from the bottom of their handouts. Give each child two small heart stickers to place over the lions' mouths. Then help children fold and staple their Bibleramas into place. (Complete instructions can be found on page 6.) Show children how to bend the tabs on the bottom of the figures and glue them to the floor of the lions' den.

Say: God protected Daniel in the lions' den, and ⭐ God protects us! Take your craft home so you can tell your family how God protected Daniel in the lions' den! But for now, let's set the crafts aside so we can make a roaring good snack!

Teacher Tip

Your "lions' den" could be a rug in the center of the room, or you could use masking tape to mark off an area of the floor. For extra fun, give each child a pair of mittens to wear as "paws" and a plastic lei to wear as a "mane." (Caution children not to pull the leis tightly around their necks or "step" on them as they crawl.)

For Extra Fun

Let children glue snippets of yarn to the lion figures as "manes."

Allergy Alert

Be aware that some children have food allergies that can be dangerous. Know your children, and consult with parents about allergies their children may have. Also be sure to carefully read food labels, as hidden ingredients can cause allergy-related problems.

Teacher Tip

If you don't have access to water, keep a supply of baby wipes for children to use.

Teacher Tip

Instead of cookies, use English muffin halves and spread them with cream cheese. If you have time, allow the children to make one treat to eat and one to take home!

Let's Eat!

Have children wash their hands. Set out the sugar cookies, paper plates, plastic knives, napkins, string licorice, prepared frosting, small candies to use for lion facial features, and candy hearts.

Let each child spread frosting on a cookie, then decorate the cookie to look like the head of a lion. Children can use the candies for eyes and noses, and licorice strings for the mouths and manes. Encourage children to place a candy heart over the licorice mouth to remind them of how God protected Daniel in the lions' den.

When everyone has finished making a snack, lead the children in a short prayer thanking God for the food. As children enjoy their treats, ask them to tell about times God has protected them or their families. After children finish eating, ask them to help clean up so they can sing some fun songs!

Let's Sing!

God Will Protect!

(Sing to the tune of "Hallelu! Hallelu!")

Hallelu, hallelu, hallelu, halleluia *(sway arms),*

God will protect! *(Pretend to zip lips.)*

Hallelu, hallelu, hallelu, halleluia *(sway arms),*

God will protect! *(Pretend to zip lips.)*

God protected Daniel! *(Pretend to zip lips.)* **Halleluia!** *(Sway arms.)*

God protected Daniel! *(Pretend to zip lips.)* **Halleluia!** *(Sway arms.)*

God protected Daniel! *(Pretend to zip lips.)* **Halleluia!** *(Sway arms.)*

God will protect! *(Pretend to zip lips.)*

In the Lions' Den

(Sing to the tune of "Mary Had a Little Lamb.")

Daniel in the lions' den, lions' den, lions' den. *(Scrunch hands to make lions' paws that are clawing.)*

Daniel in the lions' den; God protects him! *(Scrunch hands once more, then hug self.)*

When I'm feeling sad or scared, sad or scared, sad or scared *(pretend to dry eyes),*

When I'm feeling sad or scared, God protects me! *(Pretend to dry eyes once more, then hug self.)*

Let's Pray!

Before class, create a simple lion's tail out of yarn, making sure that it is long enough to hold while a child tugs on it. Simply cut the yarn into eighteen-inch lengths, braid three groups of the yarn, and leave a tassel at one end. This will be the end that children tug on during class.

Gather everyone into a prayer circle and have children repeat today's Key Verse, Isaiah 41:10a: **"Do not fear, for I am with you."** Then begin a prayer of thanks emphasizing that because he loves us, ★ God protects us. Encourage the children to think back to the beginning of the lesson when they named something that scares them. Go around the circle, and give each child a turn pulling the yarn lion's tail and asking God to protect him or her. When every child has pulled on the lions' tail, encourage children to roar to the Lord in praise!

Daniel's Tale

A long time ago in a place called Babylon, there was a man named *Daniel*. (Pause.) *Daniel* (pause) loved and served God with all his heart. *Daniel* (pause) also worked for the king of Babylon. In fact, he was one of the king's top workers. Some of the other workers were jealous of *Daniel* (pause) because he did such a good job and the king liked him so much. So they wanted to get rid of *Daniel*. (Pause.)

They went to the king and suggested that for the next thirty days, everyone should pray to the king and no one but the king. Well, the king thought that was a good idea and made it a law. And anyone who disobeyed the law would be thrown into a den of hungry *lions*! (Pause.)

Daniel (pause) liked his job and liked the king, but he knew it was wrong to pray to anyone but God. So *Daniel* (pause) kept on praying to God. Three times a day, *Daniel* (pause) got down on his knees and prayed to God, just as he had always done.

Well, that's just what those men had hoped would happen! They went and tattled to the king that *Daniel* (pause) was still praying to God. The king couldn't change the law he had made, so into the *lions'* den went *Daniel*! (Pause.) *Daniel* (pause) spent the whole night in the den with those hungry *lions*! (Pause.)

Very early the next morning, the king rushed to the den of *lions*. (Pause.) And what do you think he found? *Daniel* (pause) was fine! Here's what he told the king: "My God sent his angel, and he shut the mouths of the *lions*." (Pause.) "They have not hurt me." The king was so happy, and he made a new law that said everyone should worship the one true God!

A Fishy Prayer

Bible Story

God hears Jonah's prayer (Jonah 1–2:10).

The Point

This lesson will help preschoolers know that because he loves us, ⭐ **God listens to us.**

Key Verse

"He answered their prayers, because they trusted in him" (1 Chronicles 5:20b).

About This Lesson

In this lesson, preschoolers will learn that God loves them so much that he is always available to listen to our prayers.

Children will...

- play a fun listening game.
- learn that God will listen to them no matter where they are or what they're doing.
- create a delicious snack to help them review the story.
- think about all the different places they can talk to God.

What You'll Need

- Bible
- two-sided photocopy of the "Jonah" Collect-a-Craft handout for each child (pp. 95-96)
- glue
- safety scissors

- crayons
- pita bread
- canned frosting
- plastic knives
- small candies
- Teddy Graham cookies

Bible Background for Teacher Enrichment

Jonah was a prophet of God. God told Jonah to go to the city of Nineveh and tell the people there to stop their wickedness. But Jonah didn't want to obey God. He decided to run away and try to hide from God. So Jonah hopped aboard a ship heading in the opposite direction, toward a city called Tarshish. While out to sea, the ship that Jonah was sailing on was threatened by a storm that God had sent. The sailors were frightened and threw the cargo overboard to try to keep the ship afloat. They didn't know what else to do!

But Jonah realized that God had sent the storm because he had disobeyed

God's command. Jonah convinced the sailors to save themselves by throwing him overboard into the raging sea. Finally the sailors felt they had no choice, so they tossed Jonah overboard to what they thought would be his certain death.

But God had a plan for Jonah. God sent a big fish to swallow Jonah, thereby saving his life. Jonah remained in the fish for three days and three nights. Jonah realized that he had been wrong to disobey God, and he prayed to God from inside the fish. Jonah thanked God for saving his life and vowed to make good on God's command. Then God told the fish to spit Jonah onto dry land, and Jonah got up and headed to Nineveh!

This remarkable story can help preschoolers understand that God can and will hear us when we pray to him, anywhere and anytime!

Welcome!

Welcome the children by name, then gather everyone together. Ask children what kinds of things they like to listen to. Children might answer music, sounds of nature, the voices of their parents, television shows, movies, or laughter. Then ask the children if they think they're good listeners and begin your session with the following game.

Encourage the children to help you make a variety of noises while you read each of the following statements to them. Each child should participate in creating the sounds while you say each sentence in a normal voice. Then after each sentence, see if the children can repeat what you just said.

Some of the sounds you could encourage children to make while you talk include clapping, singing, stomping feet, and everyone singing a simple song at once. Some of the statements you could make while children are making noise include "Jesus loves you," "God listens to us," and "We can always talk to God."

Ask: • Were you able to hear what I said when you were making noise? Why or why not?

• Do you think God ever has a hard time hearing what we say to him? Explain.

Say: God never has trouble hearing what we say to him. God can hear us no matter where we are or what we're doing!

Open your Bible to 1 Chronicles 5:20b, and show children the verse.

Say: Listen to what our Key Verse says about how God listens to our prayers: "He answered their prayers, because they trusted in him." Have children repeat the verse with you several times. We can trust that God always listens to us! In today's Bible story, God even heard someone talking to him from the belly of a big fish! Let's find out more!

Bible Story Fun

Open your Bible to the book of Jonah, and show children where the book begins.

Say: Today's story comes from the book of Jonah in the Bible. Jonah was a prophet of God. Prophets were special men who God gave messages to, and then the prophets told the people what God had said. Well, one day God told Jonah to go to the city of Nineveh and tell the people there to stop being bad. But Jonah didn't want to go. He didn't like the people in Nineveh—they were mean. And Jonah was kind of afraid. Let's find out what Jonah did.

I'm going to teach you a fun rhyme to tell Jonah's story. I'll show you what motions to do. Are you ready? Here we go!

Read the following story rhyme, and lead children in the motions.

Jonah was a prophet, and he spread God's Word to all. *(Spread arms wide.)*

His job was quite important; he had a special call. *(Cup hands beside mouth.)*

Once God said to Jonah, "Go to Nineveh and speak." *(Put one finger up, then put one hand beside mouth.)*

"The people there are doing wrong; they really are quite weak." *(Shake finger and shake head back and forth.)*

Jonah didn't want to go. The people there were mean! *(Put hands on hips.)*

And so he hopped aboard a boat and hoped God hadn't seen! *(Make a rowing motion with arms.)*

But God knew right where Jonah was—he couldn't hide, you know. *(Point and shake head "no.")*

God sent a storm to rock that boat, and knock it to and fro! *(Rock back and forth.)*

The waves rose high, the wind blew hard, the sailors were afraid! *(Hug self and make a scared face.)*

Then Jonah said, "It's all my fault. Look at the mess I've made!" *(Point to self, then point all around.)*

He said to toss him overboard, though he would surely die. *(Make a diving motion overboard.)*

He felt so bad for what he'd done, and so he said, "Goodbye." *(Wave goodbye.)*

The sailors tossed him overboard and thought that he would drown. *(Hold nose and wiggle down toward ground.)*

But God sent a fish—a giant fish—to gulp poor Jonah down! *(Use entire arms to create an open "mouth," then open and close "mouth.")*

For three whole days inside that fish, Jonah sat and sat. *(Hold up one, two, and three fingers.)*

It was dark and smelly, too. Can you imagine that? *(Hold nose.)*

Jonah knew that he'd been wrong when he tried to run away. *(Run in place.)*

He wanted to apologize. He thought of what to say. *(Rub chin.)*

He thanked the Lord for saving him; he knew God loved him so. *(Hug self.)*

He vowed to go to Nineveh if God would let him go. *(Hold right hand up, palm out.)*

God heard each word that Jonah said and gave that fish a talk. *(Put hand beside ear.)*

God told the fish to spit him out so on dry land he'd walk. *(Walk in place.)*

So Jonah landed on the sand and dusted off his back. *(Dust off clothes.)*

He marched right on to Nineveh and never did look back. *(March in place.)*

If you have time, lead children in saying the rhyme several times.

Say: **God listened to Jonah's prayer, and** ⭐ **God listens to us. Right now, let's make something to help us remember today's Bible story about Jonah!**

Craft Corner

Give each child a two-sided photocopy of the "Jonah" Collect-a-Craft handout (pp. 95-96). Let children color their craft papers. Distribute scissors and glue. Let children each cut out the Jonah figure from the bottom of the page. Then help children fold and staple their Bibleramas into place. (Complete instructions can be found on page 6.) Show each child how to fold the tab on the bottom of the Jonah figure and glue it inside the scene.

Say: **When you get home you can use your craft to tell your family all about how God listened to Jonah's prayers, and how** ⭐ **God listens to our prayers. But for now, let's set the crafts aside so we can enjoy a yummy snack!**

Have children set their crafts aside until the close of the lesson.

Let's Eat!

Before class, cut pita bread circles in half. You'll need one half for each child.

Have children wash their hands. Then lead children in a short prayer, thanking God for always listening to us. Explain to children that they'll be making their own fish to remind them how God heard Jonah praying inside the big fish.

Give each child a half circle of pita bread. Tell children they can pretend that the pita bread is the fish's mouth. Set out canned frosting, plastic knives, and tiny candies for children to use as fish facial features and decorations. Then set out Teddy Graham cookies to represent Jonah. Show children how to squeeze the pita bread to make the "mouth" open and shut, and encourage children to retell the story of how God heard Jonah's prayer when he was inside the big fish.

Then let children eat their snacks. As children enjoy their snacks, ask them to think about why ⭐ God listens to our prayers. After children finish eating, ask them to help clean up so they can sing some fun songs!

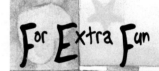

For Extra Fun

Let children glue some confetti "seaweed" and goldfish crackers inside the big fish.

Allergy Alert

Be aware that some children have food allergies that can be dangerous. Know your children, and consult with parents about allergies their children may have. Also be sure to carefully read food labels, as hidden ingredients can cause allergy-related problems.

Teacher Tip

Have children wash their hands before snack time. If you don't have access to water, keep a supply of wet wipes for children to use.

Let's Sing!

Teach children the following songs and motions to help them remember that ★ God listens to us.

God Hears My Prayers!

(Sing to the tune of "God Is So Good.")

God hears my prayers. God hears my prayers. *(Put hands beside ears, then make praying hands.)*

God hears my prayers. God hears what I say. *(Put hands beside ears, then hands beside mouth.)*

Wherever I am, wherever I am *(spread arms out at sides),*

Wherever I am, God hears what I say! *(Spread arms out and then put hands beside mouth.)*

God Hears All Our Prayers!

(Sing to the tune of "Ten Little Indians.")

One little, two little, three little prayers *(hold up one, two, and three fingers),*

Four little, five little, six little prayers *(hold up four, five, and six fingers),*

Seven little, eight little, nine little prayers *(hold up seven, eight, and nine fingers)—*

God hears all our prayers! *(Hold arms out wide.)*

Let's Pray!

Encourage your preschoolers to participate in some popcorn prayers that will remind them that we can pop up and talk to God anytime and anyplace. Begin by thanking God for always hearing us, no matter what time it is or where we are. Then let each child pop up and say a place or time they can talk to God. For example, children might pop up and say, "in the car," "at preschool," or "at my grandma's." Close the prayer by thanking God for always hearing us when we pray!

Collect-
a-Craft

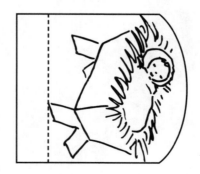

Family Discussion Starters

- How is Jesus like a gift?
- What gift can you give to God?

Family Fun

Take your child to the store to purchase a simple birthday or Christmas gift for another child—perhaps a family member or neighbor. Encourage your child to choose something he or she would enjoy having. Talk about how Jesus gave us the best gift of all when he came to earth as a baby.

Collect-
a-Craft

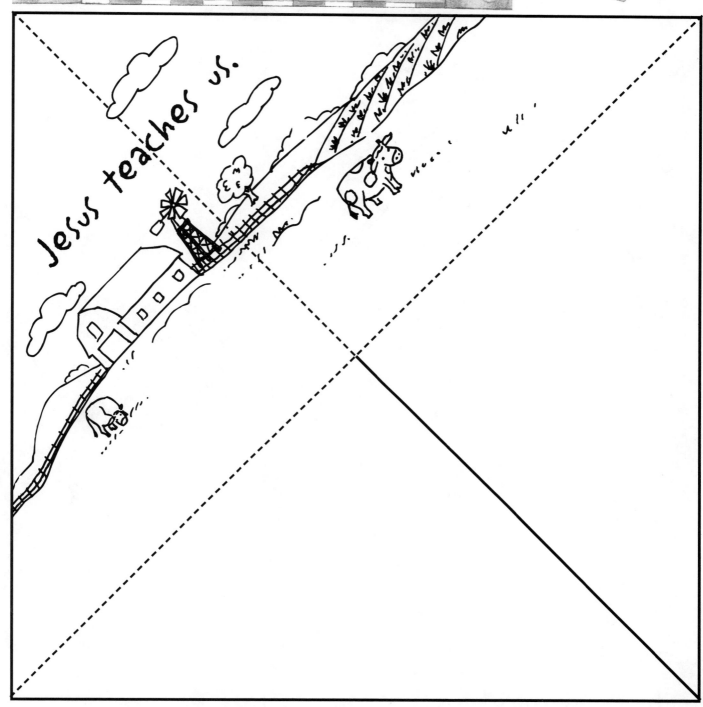

Jesus teaches us.

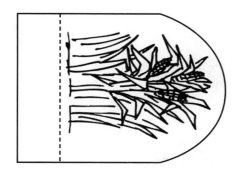

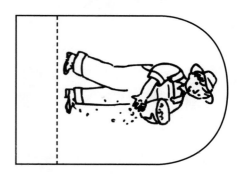

Family Discussion Starters

- What kind of soil did Jesus say seeds will grow in?
- Why is it important to learn about God?

Family Fun

Let your child "teach" you a simple game such as Hide and Seek. Then explain that Jesus teaches us so we can enjoy strong faith in the same way you enjoyed the game together.

Jesus Calms a Storm

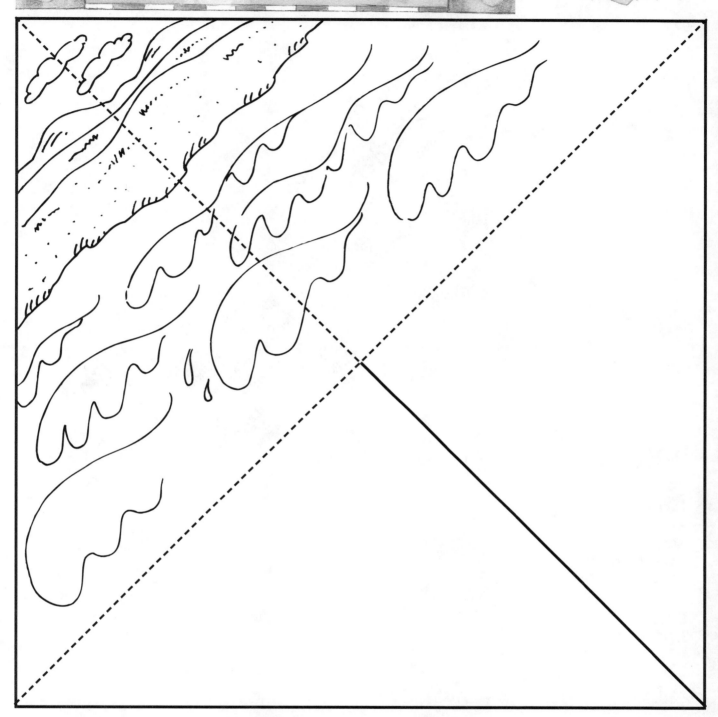

 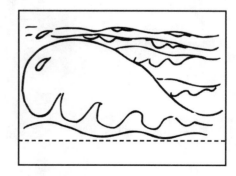

Family Discussion Starters

- What did the disciples do when they were afraid during the storm?
- What should we do when we're afraid?

Family Fun

Work together as a family to create your own story about someone who needs to trust in Jesus' protection. Take turns allowing each family member to add one sentence to the story until the problem has been established. Then discuss ways Jesus could protect the person. Conclude by reading Psalm 121:5a together.

Jesus Feeds the Five Thousand

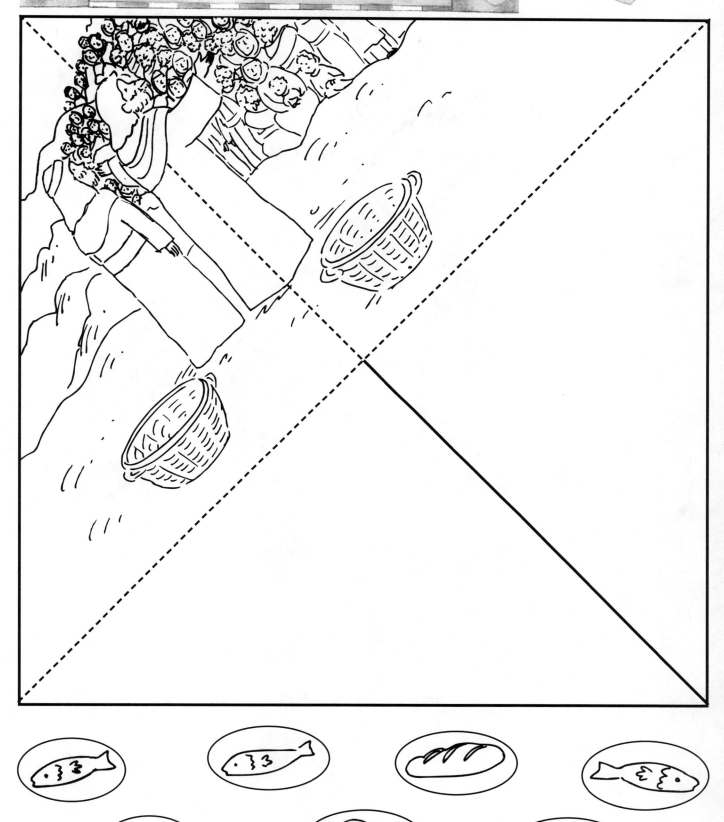

Family Discussion Starters

- How did Jesus take care of the people in the Bible story?
- How does Jesus take care of our family?

Family Fun

This week take some time to thank God for all the ways he takes care of your family. Start a list and add to it each day. For example, thank God for your home, favorite foods, love, church, and neighbors.

The Lost Son

God forgives us.

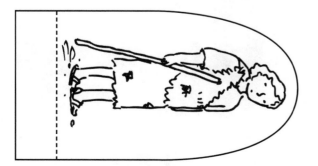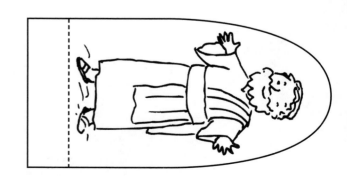

Family Discussion Starters

- Why did the father forgive his son when he came home?
- Why does God forgive us?

Family Fun

Have a Family Forgiveness Festival one night this week! Make party hats and serve fun foods to remind you of the Bible story. Serve Forgiveness Fish Sticks, I-Forgive-You French Fries, and Pigpen Pudding. As you eat, talk about how wonderful it is that Jesus forgives us!

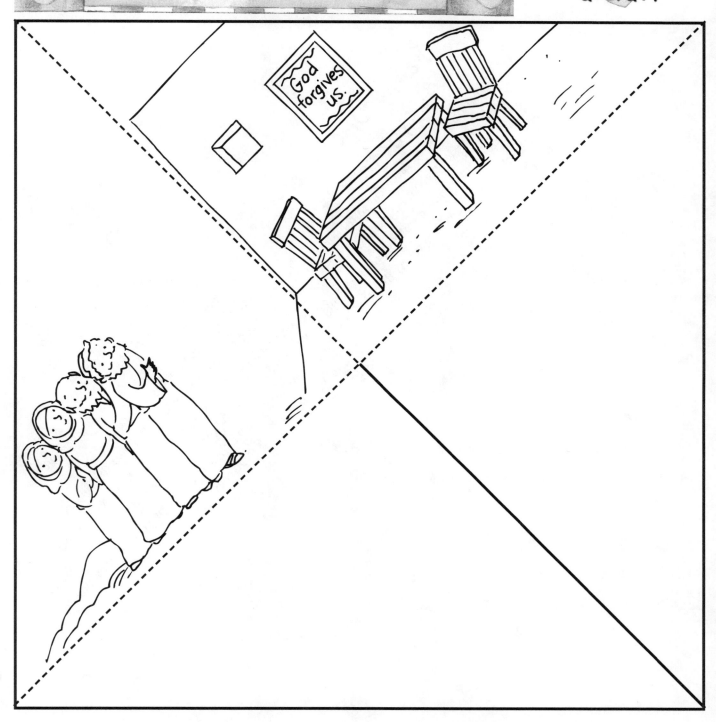

God forgives us.

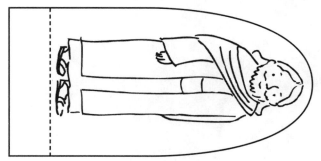

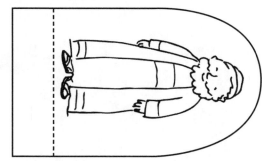

Family Discussion Starters

- What happened to Zacchaeus in the Bible story? What did he learn about forgiveness?
- How can your family members practice giving each other the kind of forgiveness that God has for us?

Family Fun

When Zacchaeus learned about how God forgave him, he gave all the money back to those he had taken it from. This week, each time you forgive someone or ask forgiveness from God or a family member put a penny in the middle of this Biblerama.

Set out some pennies in a dish near this Biblerama. Your children can place them on the floor of the Biblerama when they practice forgiveness. At the end of the week, take the coins to church and put them in the offering plate to show how thankful you are for God's forgiveness.

Jesus Died for Our Sins

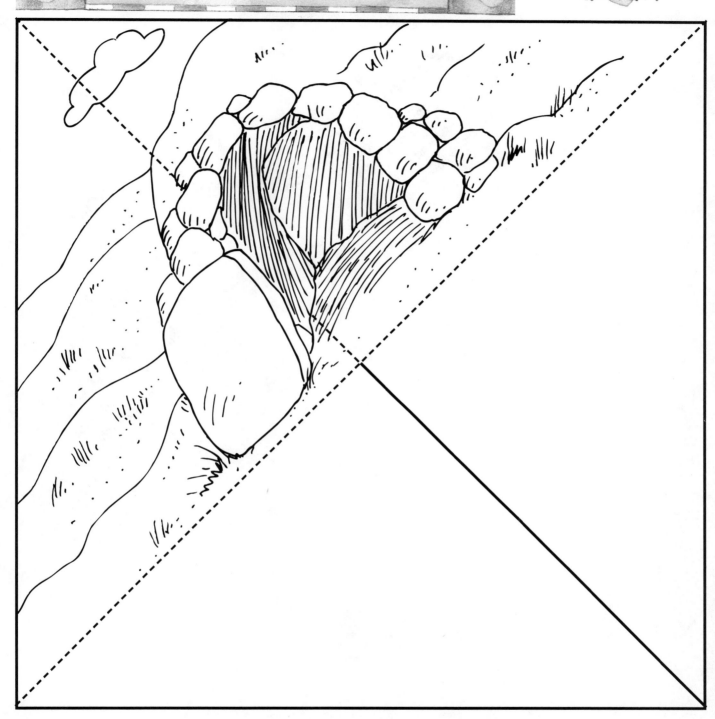

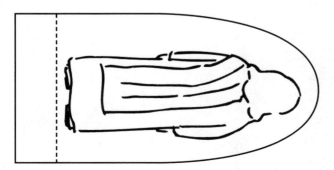

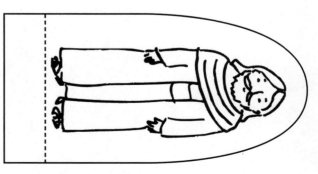

Family Discussion Starters

- Why did God send Jesus?
- Why did Jesus die on the cross?

Family Fun

Use heart-shaped cookie cutters to cut slices of bread. Then help your child spread jam on the hearts as a tasty reminder that God's love is sweet!

Creation

Family Discussion Starters

- How did God make each person in your family special?

- What's your favorite part of God's creation?

Family Fun

Take a family walk, and make a list of everything you see that God made. When you get home, enjoy a special treat of favorite foods that God made. Before you eat, pray to thank God for everything and everyone you wrote on your list.

The Ten Commandments

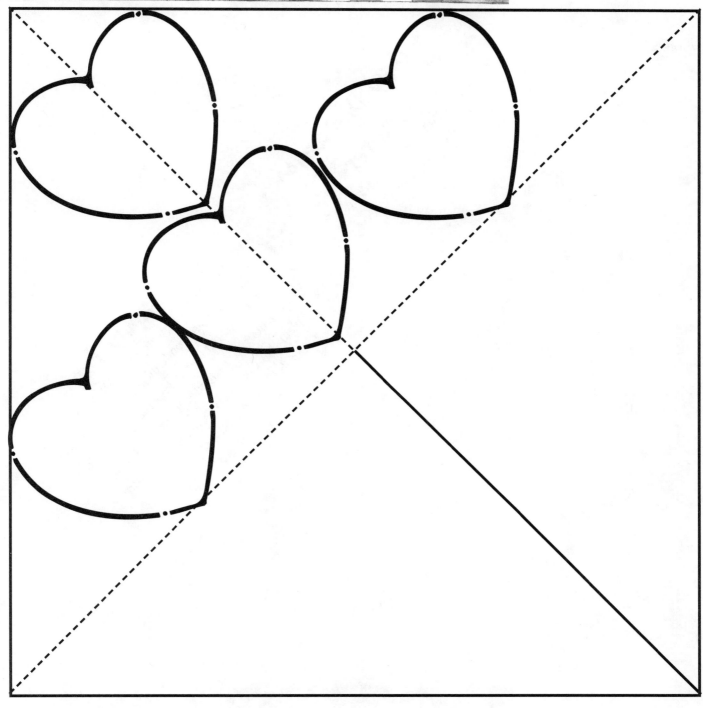

Family Discussion Starters

- Why does God give us special rules?
- Why should we follow God's rules?

Family Fun

Let your child help you prepare a simple recipe. (Cake mixes are wonderful and easy...with tasty results!) Point out that it's important to follow the instructions so the food will turn out just right. Explain that God wants us to follow his instructions so our lives will be good too!

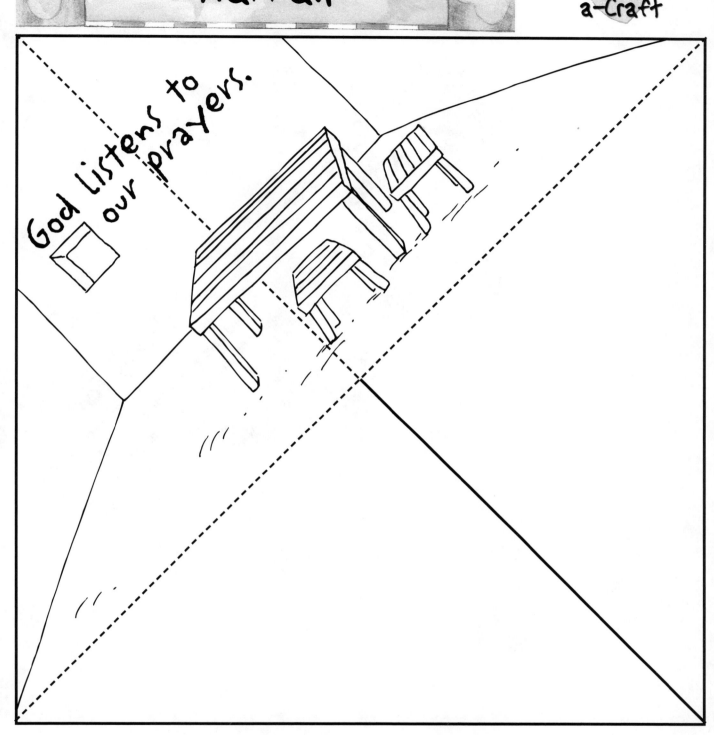

God Listens to our prayers.

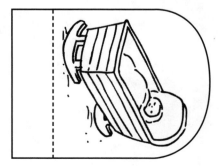

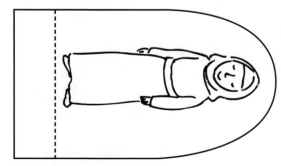

Family Discussion Starters

- What did Hannah learn when she prayed to God?
- What can our family pray to God about this week?

Family Fun

Create a prayer box at home. Decorate a shoe box and have family members put their prayer requests (in picture or word form) in the box. Every day this week, take out each request and pray to God together as a family. Remind each other that God always listens to our prayers.

Elijah

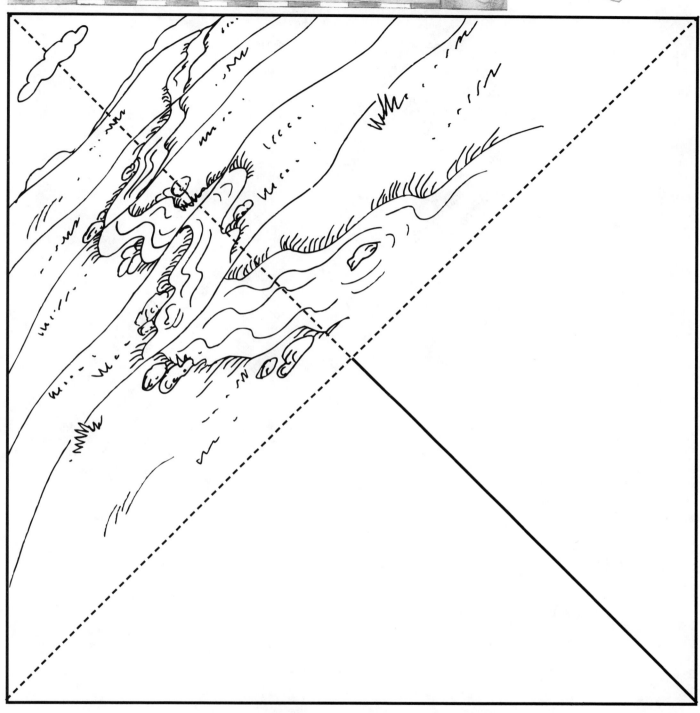

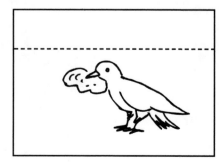

Family Discussion Starters

- When have you been really thirsty or hungry?
- How did God take care of Elijah's hunger and thirst?
- What is one way that you can remember that God has taken care of you?

Family Fun

This week, take some time to focus on all the ways God takes care of your family's basic needs of hunger and thirst. Thank God each time you are thirsty or hungry. Collect some food to take to an organization that feeds hungry people.

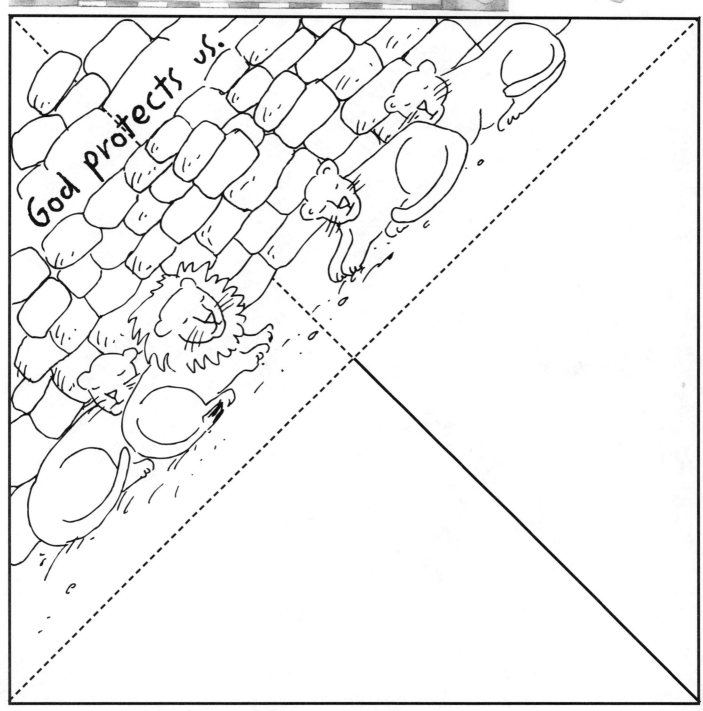

God protects us.

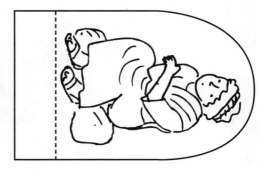

Family Discussion Starters

- How did God protect Daniel in the lions' den?
- When has God protected our family?

Family Fun

Ask each family member what struggle or trial they might be facing. Have them draw or write the struggles on slips of paper. Then every day, pray as a family as you read the papers. Ask God to protect each person, just as he protected Daniel.

Jonah

God listens to us.

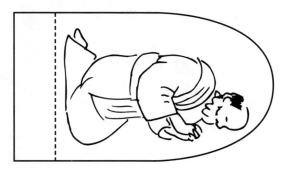

Family Discussion Starters

• What happened when Jonah prayed to God?
• When has God answered our family's prayers?

Family Fun

Say the following prayer together each night as a reminder that God will always hear our prayers, no matter where we are!

God loves us and he listens to us every time we pray.

Thank you, God, for loving us, each and every day!